T0010448

ON THE
WANDERING
PATHS

ON THE WANDERING PATHS

SYLVAIN TESSON

TRANSLATED BY DREW S. BURK
FOREWORD BY DANIEL HORNSBY

A UNIVOCAL BOOK

UNIVERSITY OF MINNESOTA PRESS
MINNEAPOLIS
LONDON

Published with the support of Villa Albertine, in partnership with the French Embassy

Originally published in French as *Sur les chemins noirs.* Copyright Éditions Gallimard, Paris, 2016.

Published by the University of Minnesota Press
111 Third Avenue South, Suite 290
Minneapolis, MN 55401-2520
http://www.upress.umn.edu

ISBN 978-1-5179-1281-9 (pb)

A Cataloging-in-Publication record for this book is available from the Library of Congress.

Printed in the United States of America on acid-free paper

The University of Minnesota is an equal-opportunity educator and employer.

28 27 26 25 24 23 22   10 9 8 7 6 5 4 3 2 1

To L.

I will walk abroad; old griefs shall be forgotten to-day; for the air is cool and still, and the hills are high, and stretch away to heaven; and the forest-glades are as quiet as the church-yard; and with the dew I can wash the fever from my forehead, and then I shall be unhappy no longer.

THOMAS DE QUINCEY,
CONFESSIONS OF AN ENGLISH OPIUM-EATER

CONTENTS

FOREWORD

Daniel Hornsby

When I was in my early twenties, my friends and I drove to the middle of Kansas (and, by extension, to the geographic center of the country) to play a concert for the richest man in town. We were idiots—we scraped money together for a tour by promising to play a house show for anyone who gave us a hundred dollars. We'd done the tour, and now it was time to pay up. The five of us packed our minivan with all our equipment in Manhattan, Kansas, where we went to school at the big agricultural university, and drove three hours west to Lorraine, where our patron lived. There, our host (think something between old Keith Richards and the human incarnation of divorce) greeted us and explained his scheme for the show. His goons would raise us on two parallel forklifts so that once we started playing we'd emerge from behind the wall enclosing his Jimmy Buffett–style saltwater pool. It was a terrible idea, but we were young and stupid and agreed to it. We hoisted up our equipment and climbed on the yoga mat–sized piece of metal, borrowed from the cattle gates that made our patron's fortune. When the time came to play, the two forklifts didn't quite sync, creating a kind of metal hiccup. We survived and played the show, which did turn out to be fun despite our teetering thirty feet above an artificial waterfall.

I spent the rest of that weekend bouncing between my friends' childhood homes. Driving through the country, I realized how far from each other people lived out there. Two of my best friends, who grew up together and attended the same tiny high school, lived almost half an hour away from one another—and that is driving at college-student speeds. (As Sylvain Tesson will soon reveal in the book you're about to read, one of the ironies of the countryside is that the bucolic heart of national mythmaking is entirely reliant on machines.) The grain elevators looked like castles on Venus, the only things crossing the barrier between the ground and sky. At night you could see every star, along with their usually hidden understudies. I grew up in exurban Indiana—my home and high school were surrounded by corn and soy, monoculture in every sense. I was no stranger to the concept of a field. But Kansas was on a different scale. Even with this hypercompression, the enormity of time is palpable. You feel about as big as a fruit fly, with the same longevity.

These rural eternities, at much lower speeds, are the subjects of Sylvain Tesson's *On the Wandering Paths.* One year after falling off a roof and seriously injuring himself, Tesson walks through the French countryside, meditating on the world around him that has also fallen and maimed itself, too. (This, I think, helped dredge up my memory of teetering on the forklift.) Tesson's concept of self and country grinds against a less than picturesque reality. You are getting old. Your world is in sad decline, too.

Tesson is rightly, pleasantly cranky. Like many of you, probably, I feel as if I've been duped. In exchange for a little convenience, we've destroyed the world and alienated ourselves from everyone. For us, Tesson offers a delightfully bitter jeremiad on globalism and decay while keeping a toe in eternity, born from a vision of a new map of the landscape. To find your own original path of thought, Tesson suggests you walk a new path through the world:

I now dreamt of a movement I would baptize as "the guild of the invisible paths." Not satisfied with simply mapping a cartographic network of physical geographical space, the invisible paths could also define the mental cartographies we would use to carve out another mode of seeking exile and withdrawal from our current frenetic age. Sketching out our cartographic movements on newly formed maps and cutting our physical movements through the serpentine pathways in the landscape, we would also simultaneously be sketching mental cartographies.

Tesson isn't romantic—this isn't an eclogue, with tipsy shepherds singing to their girlfriends. Rural life is exactly where ancient cycles of growth and death meet industrialized farming and property development. Tesson gives a clear-eyed account of his walk through the contemporary, industrialized countryside. He's something of a nineteenth-century man, a Thoreau-in-motion. An explorer who has come back from distant regions (he once made a much longer walk, a five thousand kilometer trek through the Himalayas, recorded in *La marche dans le ciel*). A Jack London type, I guess. In keeping with this, Drew Burk's translation pleasantly oscillates between more rigid nineteenth-century syntax and bright colloquial bursts.

Despite the high stakes and dark picture, there are a lot of small joys here, as when Tesson fondly describes birds as retired masters of the planet: "With their aloof way of carrying themselves, their disquieting appearance, fierce eyes, and dragon-like features, it's as if they have almost retained some memory of that former age. Sitting on their corner carpets, they must say to themselves, 'Ah, those were the days when we governed the world, sixty-five million years ago.' Will we meet the same fate as theirs?"

On the Wandering Paths places Sylvain Tesson in a long tradition of writers fleeing civilization to find something older than empire: the holy men and women of Lower Egypt, Bashō, Thoreau, and the anonymous narrator of *The Way of the Pilgrim*. It can be seen in the larger tradition of French walking literature (the works of Jean Giono, *A Philosophy of Walking* by Frédéric Gros), but it also pairs nicely with Jenny Odell's *How to Do Nothing* as part of a fresh syllabus for rejecting the world we've inherited.

By the end of the book, Tesson reminds us that the invisible paths are still out there, even in a world that seems thoroughly mapped. "We had learned at least one thing: we could still depart straight ahead in front of ourselves and struggle with nature. There were still valleys where we could fill entire days without laying our eyes on another single person to tell us which direction to take. . . . All we had to do was seek them out."

PREFACE

The past year had been rough. For a long time now, the gods had blessed the family, and we had been fortunate to bask in their sweet embrace. Perhaps some of them propped themselves up against us like fairy tales? And then suddenly their smiles turned into grimaces.

We didn't really have much of an idea about how any of this worked, but we would politely partake in this fate with an energetic ambivalence. A subtle force made its way through us with hardly the least bit of gratitude, but nevertheless left us burdened with the lightest of fatigues. Life had begun to resemble one of those beautiful paintings by Bonnard. A sun-drenched yellow permeated the white jackets and tablecloths laden with fruit cups. And a bounty of fresh air gently passed through the open windows from the adjacent orchard, where one could see children playing. Outside, the apple trees were whistling in the wind: in the end, it was perhaps the ideal decor for a good smack in the face.

And it didn't wait long to arrive. My sisters, nephews, and pretty much everyone else seemed to have been snared by one of those misfortunes that moves through the ramparts of the city like some medieval tale: a shadow slowly saunters through the narrow cobbled streets, reaching the heart of the city and, finally, the gates of the dungeon. One thing seemed clear: the plague was progressing.

My mother had died the same way she had lived, standing me up. And there I was, taken to drink, having completely wrecked myself and busted up my face while playing the fool on some roof-top. That evening I had fallen from a ledge and landed back on earth. All it took was eight meters for me to break my ribs, fracture my skull and vertebrae. Come down from the heavens, I had fallen back to the earth in a pile of bones. I deeply regretted this fall because for a long time I had been well equipped with a physical machinery that had allowed me to live a rather high-octane sort of life, always plowing full speed ahead toward the next adventure. From my perspective, a noble existence resembled something like the Siberian long-haul truck checkpoints: all the warning signs are in red, but the machine keeps on slicing its own pathway through the landscape, and the slightest Cassandra resembling a character from *The Idiot* on the side of the road waving their hands franti-cally to indicate a catastrophe ahead was simply turned into road-kill. *Robust health?* In just eight meters, I had aged fifty years.

So they picked me up off the ground, and I would come back to life. Comatose and dead, I wasn't even able to attend my moth-er's funeral or catch a glimpse of her while in heaven. A hundred billion humans have been born on this earth since the time *Homo sapiens* became what we have become. Do you really think you'll end up finding a close friend within the chaos of some eternal ant-hill teeming with cherubs?

At the hospital, everyone smiled at me. One of the wonders of the French health care system is that it never places you directly in confrontation with your responsibilities. In some past society from antiquity, they would have never extended the same level of care and attention to a drunkard as to those with much more serious illnesses. They were neither condescending nor disparag-ing. They simply saved me. Cutting-edge medical care, frequent visits from the nurses, love from my close friends and relatives, time spent reading the punkish writings of François Villon: such was the mixture required to help me heal. And first and foremost, there was one saintly being that would come visit me every day at my bedside, as if men with my affliction deserved such loyalties from other creatures: a tree outside my window that, every morning, would bestow upon me an offering of breath, a bit of its vibrating joy. Four months later, I was out of the hospital and back on my feet. Still feeling a bit rickety, with someone else's blood in my veins, my body continued to endure a great amount of pain: a dented skull, a paralyzed stomach, and a pair of scarred lungs, with a spinal column full of screws and a newly deformed face. Life was, shall we say, a bit less dancer.

For a long time, my only indulgence during those long evenings of solitude was throwing a nightly pity party for myself; such sorrow was all I could cling to. Still bandaged and bedridden, I would whisper to myself, almost out loud, "If I ever get out of this bed, I'm going to walk across the entire country of France on foot." And so it was that I began to dream. I could already picture myself walking along stone paths. My nightly reveries consisted of nothing but campfires and trampling across fields with the feet of a vagabond. The dream always came to a screeching halt when the door to my hospital room opened back up with greetings from a nurse: it was time for another fruit cup.

The doctors had given me the news: "Next summer, you can spend some time in a rehabilitation clinic and begin physical therapy." But deep down within myself I could already sense my own self-prescription taking shape. I preferred to hand over this job to the forest trails instead of simply giving in to a wheelchair: namely, the job of building back up my strength.

The next summer having finally arrived, it was now time to settle my accounts with chance. Through walking and daydreaming, traversing the countryside, I would find a way to conjure the memory of my late mother. Her ghost would reappear if I just kept my head down and stomped my way across the wooded paths for the next several months. And I wasn't simply going to walk by way of any sort of regular roads: I wanted to follow the old, hidden paths, covered over by tall grass, lined by hedges, with undergrowth of blackberry bushes, and old gravel paths linking up what now had become almost entirely abandoned villages. In spite of what certain maps might indicate, there was still another way to traverse the countryside as long as one was willing to accept taking the occasional detour and cutting one's way through the landscape. Far from the main roadways and thoroughfares, another France resided in the shadows protected from the hordes and the urban planning that often polluted any sense of mystery. A countryside replete with silence, rowan trees, and barn owls. The doctors, in their Politburo parlance, had recommended "re-education," "therapy." Rehabilitation? Therapy? Well, in my mind, that began by simply getting the hell outta there.

For a number of years now, I had already amassed a series of outlines for conquering the countryside. In what felt like almost another life, I had spoken on and on about my travels crisscrossing the world, going on one adventure after the next between Ulaanbaatar and Valparaíso. But now, in my current state, having regained my ability to walk and been given a second chance, I was suddenly struck with a revelation: it was a bit absurd that I was rather familiar with Samarkand but had never set foot in the region of Indre-et-Loire. And so it was that I would set out on a new adventure within the rural areas, the mountains and valleys, plains, and rivers of my own country, finally getting to know the one place I had always sought to leave. But there was also another, more personal reason for my adventure, and it remained scribbled on a piece of crumpled paper firmly secured in the bottom of my backpack so that I wouldn't forget.

My route traveled on foot, August 24 to November 8.

Map created by the authors of a French government report on hyperrurality. A designation of hyperrurality was given to 250 at-risk rural areas (the dark zones on the map) that had low population density and were considered to be lacking in technological services and infrastructure as well as health services and public resources. Copyright Inra UMR CESAER / M. Hilal.

1

STARTING OFF ON THE WRONG FOOT

FROM PARIS TO THE MERCANTOUR MOUNTAIN RANGE

On the Train

Why does the TGV have to travel at such great speeds? What's the point of traveling so fast? The absurdity of it all was beginning to rise up within me. Traveling at 300 kilometers per hour through a landscape that I would then traverse once again on my own two feet for the next several months! While the train continued to conquer the landscape, I thought of the people I loved and my thoughts of them held more affection than I was truly capable of expressing. Truth be told, I would rather think about them than actually hang out with them. My relatives and close friends always wanted to "get together and see each other" as if it were some sort of imperative, whereas thinking of them provided perhaps a more beautiful proximity in and of itself.

August 24, at the Italian border

My first day of walking started out from the Gare de Tende station, where I had been deposited by way of a train from Nice. I slowly headed toward the mountain passes in the distance with the feeblest of steps. Golden hues of tall blades of grass whipped in the cool night air. These initial signs of reverence within the Mediterranean landscape were an indication both of a promising friendship and a glimpse of true beauty. After months of sadness, even the gnats I could detect hovering in the sunlight were welcome omens of felicity. Their presence, in the form of a cloud at the golden hour of the day, seemed to indicate the solitude to come. One could perhaps even take it for some form of writing. Perhaps they were saying, "Are you finally going to end your war with nature?"

A very serious looking row of cedars stood tall along the path: their roots firmly planted into the slope, trees often seem rather sure of their reason for being. A shepherd was making his descent with a much more impressive stride than my own. His gnarled presence, in the bend of the path, gave him the air of a hero from one of Jean Giono's novels. Whereas I always gave off airs as if I was from somewhere else, this man clearly hailed from these lands.

"Hi, are you making your way down to the city?" I asked.

"No," he said.

"Is your flock somewhere up there in the hills?"

"No."

"Are you heading down to take a break for a bit?"

"No."

I was going to have to figure out a way to rid myself of my city habits of trying to connect through conversation.

The Col de Tende saddled the ridgeline of the Mercantour Range, forming a natural dividing line between Italy and France. I had chosen to start my journey there at the southeast corner of France and end it in the northernmost part on the cliff edges of the Cotentin Peninsula. I had learned from my travels and previous expeditions to Lake Baikal[1] that it was a Russian tradition to sit in a chair, on a tree trunk, or on the first available large rock for a couple of minutes before embarking on any sort of long journey. They would then empty themselves out, think about those they were leaving behind, worry about whether or not they had shut the stove off, hidden the body, who knows what else? So, there I sat on the beginning path leading into the mountains, in a kind of Russkie fashion, leaning against some sort of a wooden oratory or a meditating Virgin opening out onto the Italian landscape in the distance to the south and turning northward heading up into hills. I suddenly got up and began to walk.

Upon my arrival on the slopes, my weary eyes prayed for the cows as occasional rocks fell beneath the peaks. The ridges with dark bristling pines brought back memories of when I was twenty years old and had traversed the blue, serrated Chinese horizons of the Yunnan Mountains. But I quickly pushed those memories aside, letting them evaporate into the thin air of the setting sun. These jumbled sorts of analogies had become cumbersome.

Had I not already promised myself that I would abide by the proclamation found in one of Pessoa's "pagan poems":

As concerns the plant, I say "plant."
As concerns myself, I say "it's myself."
And I have nothing else to say.
What else would there be to say?

Oh, how I had my suspicions that Pessoa, *the disquiet one,* was never truly faithful to his project. How can we believe he had succeeded in being content with the world? Those who write these sorts of lines end up spending the rest of their lives betraying their own theories. During the next several weeks of walking, I was going to attempt applying a crystalline view to things without the bandages furnished by psychoanalysis or the filter of memories. Up until now, I had learned to turn nature and beings into mere pages of impressions. It suddenly appeared of the utmost urgency that I rejoice in the sun without feeling the need to evoke de Staël. To partake in the comforting embrace of the wind without citing Hölderlin. And to seek out the pleasure of a fresh glass of wine without arriving to an image of Falstaff swishing around at the bottom. In other words, I would attempt to live like one of those dogs I could make out in the distance: lapping up water peacefully with their outstretched tongues, giving off the impression that they were going to swallow up the sky whole. Swallow up the forest or the sea, or even the arrival of evening itself. Of course, almost immediately it became crystal clear that this sort of attempt was already destined for failure. A European cannot be remade.

At 2,000 meters, I detected a rather flat piece of ground to set up camp, and I made a fire close to a cement bunker. The wood was so moist, and I blew on the cinders so much to get the fire going, that my head began to spin. The warmth from the fire displaced several spiders that no longer frightened me. I had already seen a number of them out of the corner of my eye. The canvas bivvy hardly protected me at all from the spitting clouds in the darkness of the evening. It was the first night I had spent outside in fresh air since my calamitous fall. The ground welcomed me as if I had never left. This time it was a much less brutal encounter. I had finally returned to my beloved garden: a forest under the stars. The air was fresh, the ground was uneven, and the terrain was high up on a slope. Things were beginning to become enjoyable again. In those brief moments when one can cherish or aspire to them, nights spent in the outdoors are something to hold on to. A time when setting up one's camp for the evening can be experienced as the crowning achievement after a long day of movement. Jotting down such brief moments of respite provided the warmth of a blanket and dilated our dreams. One can forgo awaking to the clamor of the cities and breathe in deep: Fresh air! Fresh air! One year earlier, while lying in a hospital bed, I had dreamt of sleeping under a canopy of trees. And now the time of campfires had returned.

August 25, in the valley of the Roya

The previous night had been rather strange. It began around 11 p.m. I suddenly heard gunfire about 200 or 300 meters away from me and then again, and then a series of detonations continued throughout much of the rest of the night, sometimes with only thirty seconds between each round. Who could be firing off rounds out here in the middle of the night? Was there a deranged monk nearby fighting it out with the shadows?

As I made these first moves in my journey, gently maneuvering my way through the landscape, I told myself that if I ended up finally making my way across the entire country, I'd chalk it up as a remission in my human condition. If I didn't make it, I'd consider it a complete relapse. The perspectives of a cure were rather slim and off in the distance! As far away as the Cotentin Peninsula! I placed my salvation in nothing else but movement.

In the morning, I came across a shepherd's quarters in a hollow. There I found a slender woman with rosy Flemish cheeks and bare biceps in the midst of working the ground. As if she had come right out of a Brueghel painting and had immediately begun taking up her trade.

"I heard quite a few rounds of gunfire last night," I said.

"Ah, that was a gas engine, used to scare off the wolves. Boom! Boom!" she explained. "What do you want?"

"What do you have for sale?"

"Dry cow's cheese."

"I'll take three hundred grams. Are the wolves really scared off by the engine noise?"

"I don't really know. That'll be three euros."

Things had nevertheless gone a bit sideways. People multiplied and invested in a world. They cemented over the earth, occupied the valleys, populated the plateaus, killed all the gods, and massacred the wildlife. They had abandoned entire generations of their offspring on these grounds along with their flocks of genetically modified herbivores. One day, thirty years ago, making its way through the Abruzzes, a wolf returned to the Mercantour Region. Certain minds got it in their head to protect it. The shepherds became furious since the presence of a wolf meant that they had to take turns staying up all night on watch. "The friends of the wolf sleep in warm beds in the city," the farmers complained. And now, it seems we had even arrived at a point where they had to install machines in alpine meadows imitating gunfire to protect the herbivores from the wild animals that had simply returned to their homes. I would rather be a wolf, I thought to myself: "Progress? What a farce."

August 26, leaving Mercantour

The evening was already beginning to cast its shadows over the landscape, and I was still attempting to slowly regain my strength. At the moment, I wasn't exactly making great strides. Three days among the rocky paths had already taken a toll on my back. "What's the point of dragging this tattered sack of bones across an entire country that lay in ruins?" I began to wonder as my eyes zoomed in on two chamois in the middle of cleaning themselves. A mother and son amid a chaos of rubble. I was curious as to how many humans were also a bit envious of animals. The little one had come hurtling at me and brushed against my leg behind one of the rocks. He had hesitated for a couple of seconds. During the eighteenth century in the Virgin Islands, wild animals would eat right out of the hands of European explorers before receiving a musket blow to the head in celebration of this human encounter. The little chamois had at least made a healthy U-turn, realizing that perhaps I wasn't a creature recommended for frequent visitations.

As I walked past a green lake, I came across a waterfall, and cascading through its froth, I set forth back up toward the high peaks. I made my way north past Mont Bégo, now deserted by its prehistoric spirits, and my reading of *Knulp* had finally stopped bringing me down. Hermann Hesse had created a vagabond who walked through a friendly German countryside rendered all the more sweet thanks to the golden allures of autumn. Sure, good old Knulp eventually ended up dying alone, but at least before paying a heavy price for his aesthetics of irresponsibility he had provided the villagers a glimpse of another form of noble life in the form of flânerie. If I wanted to continue walking in a dreamlike splendor, with benevolent thoughts at my side, I'd certainly need to find some pints of beer with their foam heads spilling over onto wooden tables.

At the Pas de Colomb, in a tiny valley, sat the small church of the Madonna de Fenestre. In France, one often finds religious sites dedicated to the Virgin Mary in caves as well as at various water sources. The Virgin Mary had pretty much monopolized all the strangest sites on the map. I once even encountered a "Notre-Dame des Falaises"—Our Lady of the Cliffs—on the edges of Cape Canaille. Such religious artifacts were how the Catholic faith was able to retain a bit of the ancient paganism from another age, a way of not entirely cutting its ties with the former spirits of the land.

There I sat, resting in the shade under the vaults of the church. On the walls one could make out remnants of the votive offerings left by alpinists who had been rescued from a fall. It was their climbing ropes that had saved them, but it was perhaps preferable to think of it in terms of Heaven's grace. Upon entering on the left, one could see that a fairly new stele had been added, in memory of Hervé Gourdel, a mountain guide, a child of the Vésubie River, who had been murdered by fanatics the year previous. In my hospital bed, I had been haunted by his martyrdom. I had imagined the alpinist, tied up with his head covered, handed over. I had taken to sharing a kind of fraternity with Gourdel. And on this evening, his memory rose back to the surface.

On one of the columns of the church, one could make out a plaque mentioning the decapitations of a group of Knights

Templar. Was this the work of invaders who are said to have destroyed sanctuaries around these same regions?

And on this night, as I rolled around seeking sleep in my canvas bivvy, I saluted the mountain guide Gourdel, before letting the froth of my thoughts dissolve into dreams. A cow, no doubt preoccupied with other things, could be heard outside "mooing" her own requiem in the darkness of the alpine pasture.

2

OF RUINS AND BRAMBLES

INTO THE MOUNTAINS AND VALLEYS OF HAUTE-PROVENCE

August 27, the Vésubie and Tinée Rivers

The valleys unfurled, the villages came and went. The stones continued to roll even more onto the limestone paths of Haute-Provence. One evening at Saint-Dalmas, as I began to feel the grinding of the screws and steel planted in my back, I caught a glimpse of one of those vacation cottages, a *gîte*. Oh, how I wished I had lived during that long-forgotten era when the following dialogue could have taken place:

"Do you have a place for me to sleep for the evening? A roof and some straw would suffice."

"We can offer you some wine and bread if you can help us with the hay baling."

But really, one had to have truly hit one's head pretty good to start dreaming up those sorts of conversations! We were no longer living in the times of Knulp, after all. You poor bastard, I told myself, when a woman with long flowing brown hair explained to me as I walked up to the front desk: "We would have loved to have provided you the discounted rate for a regular *gîte d'étape,* but we don't have the administrative accreditation." I was going to have to be a bit more crafty if I was going to find a way to avoid, if only for a brief moment, having to continuously submit to the administrative rules of the country. Would it even be possible for me to discover any remaining territories that hadn't been completely subjected to the politics of territory?

One of the former prime ministers of the Fifth Republic (Jean-Marc Ayrault—during the period of Anatole France) had ordered the creation of a report on the management of the French countryside. The written report was eventually published during the period of another minister (Manuel Valls—during what we could refer to as the Offenbach era of the theatricality of the French political sphere), bearing the title *Hyperrurality*. A battery of experts—specialists of the unverifiable—judged that at least thirty or so French departmental regions could be classified under this banner of "hyperrurality." For them, the notion of "rurality" was not a form of grace but a veritable curse: the report complained of the backwardness of these areas that had not yet been brought into the digital world, whose open landscape had not been completely cleared away by a network of highways, and whose villages had not been urbanized enough, or that found themselves deprived of those precious big-box shopping centers and that lacked administrative access. What some of the rest of us quixotic idiots considered vital for engaging in a certain relation to paradise on earth—a bit of wildness, preservation, and isolation—were considered categories of underdevelopment according to the aforementioned report.

The report had provided a bit of reassurance. The authors were certainly confident prophets: "Hold on just a bit longer, our fellow citizens of the back country, we are coming to bring you progress!" Thanks to the State, modernity would soon be flowing through the fallow backwoods. Wi-Fi access would magically bring all the country bumpkins up to speed and in line (or perhaps I should say *online*) with the norms. Instead of writing "*Pars les champs et pars les grèves,*"[1] future Flauberts would be able to retort

with sayings like "Through the ZUP and the ZAC."[2] The benefi-
ciaries of these management plans would become good soldiers
of urbanity, a replaceable citizenry, shielded from any form of
what the report referred to as "radical votes." That was truly what
was in the back of the minds of those who created the report: to
ensure some kind of a psychic conformity of these so-called impossible people.

Among the battery of measures to be considered, the report
listed things such as *the right to the pursuit of successful experimentations to help modernize equality in salary.* What was the application
of such strange language? What were the lives of the authors who
wrote such phrases nourished off? Did they have any sense of the
small pleasure one could procure from wiping one's mouth on the
side of the collar of one's jacket after a gulp of a glass of wine from
the Savoie, the pleasure of lying down in a grassy field while the
silhouette of a bird could be seen flying in the sky overhead?

The text of the report was illustrated with a number of maps
of the departments deemed as *hyperrural*; the maps showed a
large dark zone the government prepared to fly over providing
aid. (*State intelligence at the service of hyperrurality* was the name
these troubadours gave to their initiative!) This dark zone in-
cluded the entirety of the Southern French Alps, and then continued on toward the Vosges and the Ardennes, basically enveloping
the entire Massif Central and a number of neighboring departments of the Haute Loire. Only a couple of weeks later in my
exploratory reading would I learn that all these so-called hyperrural territories—from the Mercantour Mountain Range to the
Lozère—corresponded almost exactly to the movements of the
wolf population as it slowly reestablished itself in France. Not a
crazy move by the wild beast! It considered tranquility to be one
of its highest virtues. Not only did wolves not have a tendency to
attack humans, they did everything they could to avoid them.

At the hospital, riven with back pain, contemplating these
maps, I found that the outline of the route of my adventure was

slowly beginning take shape. In his 123rd fragment, remaining as obscure as ever, Heraclitus states his famous proclamation: "Nature loves to hide." Like incomplete beings, I had always harbored a penchant for remote places. As I dreamt of these so-called regions of "hyperrurality," I knew they would be my chance to look forward to something. And I held one of the maps from the report up against my heart as if it were a photo of my fiancée. The map held the promise of escape. My route would not be sketched out throughout the entirety of the hyperrural zones. Once I had exited the Massif Central, I would shift my bearings toward the Northwest in order to eventually arrive at the English Channel. My journey would culminate on the cliffs of Le Havre, right at the point where land finally gave way to the sea, thereby offering up a chance to make a quick U-turn or move onward with an angel's leap out into the oceanic depths. In my eyes, cliffs had always made for good borders.

I reviewed my plans. I had my objective: seek out the wilderness areas and the uncultivated territories. My route had been sketched out and I already had the requisite maps thanks to the reports from the urban land rejuvenation studies conducted by the State. I knew how to get around because I considered walking to be its own general form of medicine. It would be the very key to my recovery. Quite simply, among all the adventures I had embarked upon, none were as well-organized as this one.

Looming over the hills of the Tinée River, nestled on a mountain spur, was the village of Marie. Marie also happened to be the name of my mother, and I derived a bit of pleasure in thinking that her soul perhaps decided to make a brief rest stop here.

At the open-air washbasin, a woman stood. Was she in the midst of contemplating the ravages of time reflecting back up from the water?

"I'm Dedette. I'm eighty years old. I was born here. I live here and I plan on staying here!"

I withheld from Dedette the fact that the report on hyperrurality spoke of a *mobile* France, *connected* and *modern*. One could almost hear the voices of civil servants whispering, "Farewell, Dedette!"

I made my way down toward the Var by way of a path perched on the right bank of the Tinée. It was the ancient donkey path from Nice to Barcelonnette. These days, the mules no longer traveled along this path. They now resided in the ghostly shadows for a people who, in just one century, had taken over the valley and left the brambles behind them.

Farther along, as I arrived at the village of Clans, I discovered my arrival coincided with the annual town festival: among a myriad of tents one could sense a bit of underlying restlessness. Instead of simply pinching some shepherds while blaring out songs with voices distorted by a significant quantity of *pastis,* they had organized an entire day around the *Star Wars* films. I enjoyed watching the gentlemen decked out as Darth Vader frolicking around underneath the sycamore trees. And then I continued on my way. One doesn't walk all the way from the Italian border to the Tinée River simply to watch a parade of robots. And the switchbacks in the paths plunging toward the river created a beautiful shimmer of light reflecting off the slope. In Provence, the trails all seemed to give off airs of fleeing snakes.

August 30, the Haute Vallée of the Var

I reached the banks of the Var around noon, passing by the flooded area of the river. Astonishingly, the water was waist high. I searched through the thicket, trying to uncover a path that would lead me back up into higher elevation. I got lost in the hills with no outside patio seating in sight. I spotted a trickle of animals that served as a modest trail, the tiniest and most mysterious trail on the scale of nomenclature for paths—the last resort for someone walking out in the landscape. The brush closed in back around me, and I once again settled back onto the pebble paths of the banks of the river. After ten hours of walking during a heat wave, I had actually covered a distance of only twelve kilometers! How did I procure a taste for such painful wanderings? Perhaps from the very pleasure derived in simply completing them.

When such worries began to weigh me down, I reflected on the image of who I was one year earlier. Getting shipped around in the hospital from one specialist to the next, a body in pieces, crammed full of tubes. And then, I recalled the first shudder of life, in taking my first step, all by myself, outside of the hospital room, out into the corridor, and it was as if I had climbed to the top of the Aiguille Verte via the Whymper Couloir. And the darkness began to dissipate. There is an expression common to Russian drunkards: "Tomorrow will be worse than today." I used to hold on to such expressions. Since my fall, I've penetrated into the depths of myself, leading me to accept the contrary: "Things will get better."

For the moment, I was in the midst of battling it out with some unruly, anarchic shrubs on the slopes. Traversing through a patch of wilderness provided the occasion to disappear a bit—a noble fantasy. In trampling through the fallen trees, following alongside the ravines, one walked across islands of silt and mud and in so doing, one found a modicum of escape.

My accidental fall had led to a number of concerned eyes focused on me. Friends, doctors, relatives, specialists, administrators—each in their own way offered to control me. Even a specialist in addiction had offered to get me back on my feet. My time spent with him only led me to feel somewhat as if I had experienced the era of prohibition (the prohibition of living as much as I stupidly understood it). In the end, I had thanked him for his effort in discreetly expressing my fear of actually acquiring perhaps a slight taste for his profession. Once I left the hospital, the overall generalized surveillance only doubled. And our ordinary lives became more exposed on screens, reduced to statistics, slowly becoming freeze-dried within the cybernetic

Of Ruins and Brambles

plumbing, taking root within electronic chips and plastic cards. Were we merely born to feed piles of digital documents?

Struggling my way through the brush along the Var River certainly led to some painful lacerations on my legs, but at the very least it allowed me to escape a bit from the photoelectric stack that scrutinized our existences. The gaze of the all-seeing *eye* was no longer staring directly at me. Fleeing in this manner provided me with a dual virtue: a way of healing and a way of forgetting.

It was worth reminding myself, however, that I was almost deprived of such graces, having avoided permanent paralysis by several thousandths of a millimeter. Not being an adherent of the Christian idea that one's trials or tribulations, one's life struggles, are gifts from the heavens, I would have drawn from them a certain affliction. My life in a wheelchair would have been utterly unimaginable. Having regained the use of my legs, I no longer could cling to despair. My freedom of movement having once again been restored, I could now scramble along as soon as the shadow of a constraint, request, or a summons appeared—or worse: the sound of a telephone ringing. Bernanos's instincts were accurate when he stated at the beginning of *Français, si vous saviez,* that "there is no longer a large quantity of freedom in the world, that is clear, but there is still a great deal of space."

Space! It still offered up its folds to anyone who wanted to kneel down in front of the maps and partake of communion with their force. Currently, on the limestone ridge and later, on the granite bedrocks, I compulsively unfolded and scanned the pages of my printed-out maps. These regional maps were pure wonders. One could derive a certain pleasure from having such a detailed layout of an entire region. For the moment, I had ten different such maps in my backpack to help me advance all the way to Mont Ventoux. They provided insight into the lesser paths, the unknown back roads deep in the heart of the Acropolis, unknown paths and forest service roads by which one could disappear. I could never stare at these representations of the landscape scaled down to 1:25,000 without wondering who was out there, wandering along under my fingertips, on the edge of an isolated road, on the zigzagging trail of a slope. And who exactly lived in this house indicated in the middle of a huge terrain? An ogre? A former dancer? Maps are gateways into an entire world of dreams.

These traces marked by stars and the various dotted lines were rural trails, pastoral paths that had been recorded by the land registry, forest service roads, secondary roads deep at the edges of regions, and ancient routes—*viae*—that were hardly maintained, often on private lands, and often left solely to the wanderings of farm animals. The entire map was replete with the veins of these arteries. They were my *invisible paths*. They opened up onto the possibility of evasion and escape from the everyday. They were forgotten paths where silence reigned and one would never encounter another human being. And where an opening and passage through the woods would often just as quickly lead to another dead end. Certain individuals hoped to enter into History. We were the ones who simply wanted to disappear into the geography of the landscape.

Secret passageways, invisible paths retaining a memory of a former country where traveling was at one time only done on foot, these were the networks of a once entirely rural land. These paths didn't belong to those so-called hiking trails, those well-groomed trails, bolstering a myriad of signs used by the local runners and other health-conscious folk. Even when these paths were close to an urban area, the map at 1:25,000 scale posed some problems: a sudden rise in the terrain, a discrete slope or passageway. Where the shadows lingered, there was always the possibility of survival. Even in the heart of the urban areas, there remained trickling paths to be found carved into the landscape. If foxes and ferrets were still capable of finding their way into the heart of European cities by way of ditches and counterscarps, we could just as easily maintain our balance on these fine invisible threads. Linking these paths throughout the countryside certainly slowed down my movements, but it also bestowed on me some advantages: not having to inflict myself with traversing the suburbs so as to avoid the potential simmering of roasting tarmac.

In the 1980s, René Frégni, a writer from Provence, published a novel about a military deserter hunted throughout the highways of Europe. It was a striking work with the title *Les chemins noirs* (The dark paths). *These would be my invisible paths. Imperceptible paths.* The paths I would travel so as to remain hidden from the traces of modernity and urban architecture. From the very beginning of my journey, I struggled with my collection of maps to trace a sinuous route so that I could remain incognito. Not because I was on the run from the authorities, like the character in Frégni's novel, but rather because I felt something of a freedom of movement and a true inhalation of fresh air that could only be breathed along these back roads and passageways. The first test I would have to overcome was creating such a journey amidst a countryside of trails that had now been reduced to mere fragmentary paths. This exercise in land surveying had become much harder than I had expected: one had to set aside a great deal of time to accurately create one's itinerary. It led to a rather tiresome affair for my eyes.

· · ·

I had suddenly become obsessed with a dream. I now dreamt of a movement I would baptize as "the guild of the invisible paths." Not satisfied with simply mapping a cartographic network of physical geographical space, the invisible paths could also define the mental cartographies we would use to carve out another mode of seeking exile and withdrawal from our current frenetic age. Sketching out our cartographic movements on newly formed maps and cutting our physical movements through the serpentine pathways in the landscape, we would also simultaneously be sketching mental cartographies. It would not be a gesture of contempt for the world at large nor would it bear the audacity of attempting to change it.

No! Its modest aim would purely and simply be a manner of no longer having anything in common with it. This simplest gesture of avoidance would be, in our current horizon of reverie, a blissful marriage of vital force and elegance. And orchestrating this withdrawal suddenly seemed of the utmost urgency. The rules of this existential invisibility would give way to a series of imperatives: don't fret over the frenetic convulsions of current affairs, restrain one's anger and anguish, carefully choose what one gets upset over. Select one's refined tastes wisely as well as one's disgust or nausea; remain only between walls composed of books and forest trails, seated around tables of friends, remembering in death only those whom one loved, surrounding oneself with one's family and friends, lending help to others based on a recognition of their humanity and not merely on carefully studied statistics. Basically: turn away from the madness. Even better: disappear. "Live hidden," said the great Epicurus in one of his maxims (and it's only because he was somewhat successful in this tactic that we still remember him two thousand years after his death). In his own manner, Epicurus had already provided his own outline for *the guild of invisible paths.*

We would suddenly find ourselves to be great in numbers on these invisible, much lesser paths since there were already a great many who had grown weary or developed an allergy to the realm of virtual illusions. The current era's slogans had certainly worn us down: *Enjoy! Take care! Be connected! Be safe!* We had become nauseated by the neon blinking shine of the cityscape. If we merely trampled over our pallid high-tech-screen lives and continued our way forward, we would suddenly find our way onto another trail. An invisible path would open up wide in front of us and beneath our feet. A tiny shimmering light at the end of the matrixial tunnel. All this reverie was not some sort of political agenda, it was merely an open invitation: *to get the hell out of town.* To live suddenly appeared to me as synonymous with a *form of escape.* During the long slog back to Paris after the battle at Berezina,

Napoleon had made the following diagnosis to one of his generals, Caulaincourt: "There are two types of men—those who command and those who obey." At a certain point earlier in my youth, when I had become obsessed with and passionate about everything concerning the history of Empire—to the point of taking a bath wearing a classic bicorn helmet—I had certainly concurred with this statement. Today, however, as I carefully trudge over the muddy, silt-laden path of the Var trying not to get my shoes stuck, I'm of the opinion that the dear old emperor had forgotten a third column in his anthropological description: men who flee. "Sire!" I would have yelled out to him, if I had made his acquaintance. "Sire! Fleeing is also a form of commanding! At the very least, it's the one mode of taking command of one's destiny so as not to have someone else's grip on you."

. . .

The next morning, as I passed through Entrevaux, I would begin to make my way up into the plateaus. Once I was able to reach them, everything would be fine. I would have to delicately balance on the razor's edge of the ridgeline. One is always a bit more at ease on the edge; one carefully and slowly moves one foot in front of the other with the most delicate of movements. The sky begins to extend its hand in friendship, but one is also at a greater risk of experiencing the slightest drop in elevation as if receiving an incurable wound.

Later that evening, still making my way across the Var—but now over a small handmade bridge—I learned that the civic work in question had been "built in 2006 by M.E.***." Another characteristic of the nobility of those traversing the invisible paths: no one leaves their name.

August 31, in the countryside of the Verdon

Finally, I had arrived at those great heights providing a subsequent bounty of fresh air and giving way to even larger, open strides through the landscape. It took only three days for me to reach the Valensole plateau by way of a thin relief of rounded hilltops, between the Var and Verdon.

I passed through Castellane, slowly closing in on Moustiers, and when I arrived I would toss my bivvy out underneath a carefully selected tree for the night: either a green oak or a conifer. Such tree cover served as both a source of shelter and shade as well as forming a natural umbrella from any possible incoming precipitation. The screws in the steel plate now lodged in my back forced me to sleep on my side. My inflatable sleeping pad provided a modicum of cushioned support, but any time I turned and made contact with the ground, I suddenly missed the comfort of the hospital bed. Sleep was late to arrive and the trees trembled in the wind, but not out of fear. It was more of a whimpering sigh, a slight worry, a palpable doubt that the sun would perhaps never return, as the shadows of the night set in. I suddenly recalled the lands of the Berber tribes in the Atlas Mountains. People who withdrew into the mountains had created a sumptuous expression to delineate the nomads from sedentary populations. The former were given the name "men of light," with their hardened, leathery skin, baked by the sun, and their ceaseless battle with the wind making their beds under the rooftop of the heavens. The latter were "men of the shadows" who sought shelter under tiled rooftops and whose unsettling dreams never left the four walls of their houses. My nights sleeping under the tree canopy were nights spent in the company of the sun.

As I rose from my bivvy, the pleasure of the rays of sunshine coming into contact with the skin were akin to the first moments of settling into a warm bath. The alpine pastures whose vegetation had been slowly peeled away by centuries of pastoral contact covered the high reliefs. Alpine hikers adorned in Gore-Tex would occasionally cross my path and make their way through these parts. In the distance, fluorescent petals bounced about in the wind. The only creatures remaining to bear witness to the mysteries of life were a few grasshoppers and several birds of prey drifting high across the sky. The birds were correct to carefully track their targets like the vultures in an old Sergio Leone film, since our world is basically on the brink of death. They probably viewed it as nothing more than a buffalo carcass.

There were also lizards by the handful that slithered their way among the stones and rocks at the slightest cause for alarm. Their ancestors had once been the lords of the earth. The dinosaurs once ruled the earth before their sudden disappearance at the end of the Cretaceous Period. These tiny guardians of the shadows were the distant inheritors of the former masters of the world. With their aloof way of carrying themselves, their disquieting appearance, fierce eyes, and dragon-like features, it's as if they have almost retained some memory of that former age. Sitting on their corner carpets, they must say to themselves, "Ah, those were the days when we governed the world, sixty-five million years ago." Will we meet the same fate as theirs? We seem to be leading the dance at this moment, acting as the regents of the chain of life. While we traffic in atoms, modifying genes, augmenting reality with chips of silicon, we are also recomposing the initial poem of existence. But as for the future? Power alone is not enough to endure. Lizards are the living reminders of this. Perhaps we will simply move into the background, away from our place at the center stage of life. Perhaps several of us, slightly diminutive in stature, will survive in the shadows so as to recall a once glorious past, like those scaly former sons of the gods, the lizards.

I paid my respects to the ruins I came across on my journey and never forgot to carefully visit them. Most of the time, they were merely former sites of a preceptory or some sort of commandery looming at the top of the plateaus. Such sites had once presided over the fates of a bucolic society. But the postwar period had rung in the era of an exodus back down into the foothills. All that remained were these half-broken bits of wall firmly rooted in yellowed, grassy fields. They were rather attractive sites. Each crumbling enclosure I came upon held an opportunity for a rest break. There was something precious about these withdrawn zones, demarcated by harrowed patches of blackberries. Each beach of silence was worth its weight in gold. Geographers had invented a wonderful expression to describe the phenomena of abandoned villages at high altitudes in Provence: *déperchement*—uproosting—to abandon one's perch. Such an exodus had begun during the first industrial revolution and the peasant bloodbath of the war of 1914 followed by the subsequent industrialization of the country during the twentieth century. After World War II, the high limestone plateaus quickly lost population density. The winds of "the Glorious Thirty" swept up the farmers from their foothills and carried them down gently toward the plains and even toward the cities. These peasant farmers dreamt of an easier and less stone-laden existence. Life became a bit more replete with comfort, and their children no longer knew a life of dirt and toil. Through the creative form of the novel, Jean Giono had discovered a way for reimagining a renewal of the countryside so as to rejuvenate the village, but most of the time the villagers fled the landscape in the manner of a combat unit fleeing an enemy's counterattacks. When a mountain region becomes modernized, humanity begins to flow downstream like a brook. And the valley, suddenly stricken with Alzheimer's, no longer has any memory whatsoever of the fact that the mountains were once harbingers of life. Could I entertain the notion that these very slopes once resonated with the vibrations of the cries of donkey-drawn carriages? The past leaves no echo. In only a half century, the acceleration and hypertrophy of human systems—cities, nations, societies, businesses—had imposed a new musical theory onto the valleys. *Size and speed* were the new foundations upon which the twenty-first century was to be constructed. Agitation and excess are never good news. There was nevertheless a consolation: if we were to consider that the great flux was the only law governing life and that History had no meaning whatsoever, and that we were embarking on a ghost train without any hope of slamming on the brakes, or changing its direction, we could perhaps still seek out another way via these paths. All it required was to resume this long walk and extend our greetings to the small number of wildlife that presented themselves during our travels.

So, I continued to wander in silence, among collapsed barns and abandoned farms, alongside paths that had been reconquered by vegetation. "Of Ruins and Brambles": it would make a great title for a long, sweeping monograph on the high plateaus of Provence. There would be no one left to cry out to in the cottages since such structures no longer remained.

Stretched out on the grass, high above an agricultural region that the map designated as the Maurels, I contemplated the limestone strata. They seemed to convulse in an undulatory pattern. Throughout my various adventures trekking around the globe, I had learned that a landscape is never merely strange, but sometimes it can be viewed as being drunk. Tortured by the various spasms of its folds, it becomes mad. Tectonics are the very opium of landscape.

On the plateau, I had already begun to partake of the nectar of these days of arid intoxication. Baking in the solar oven, the limestone continued to flourish. The rocky ground provided shelter for plants specializing in survival, bouquets of unknown heroines.

The pleasure I retained from my time in the plateaus was nourished and coincided with the slow return of my health. Healing is derived from a vegetal process: health is distributed throughout the organism like plant fibers. It begins to climb and grow. My personal care plan was to simply let it run its course through the continual pleasure of the mezza voce of a moderate effort of my continual movement of walking. The daily ritual of setting back out on the paths provided an enjoyable, low-intensity practice that could be summarized in the following way: detect any traces of life in the mountains, the beauty found in the gaps of an inlet, the sighting of a Provençal farmhouse or remnants of Roman architecture. A nighthawk suddenly shot out right in front of me. It was something I'll never forget. I would jot down several lines in my notebooks on any occasion when the spectacle of an oak in a golden field aroused in me some sort of affectionate greeting by way of the flapping of one of its branches in the wind. Walking was akin to fishing. Hours of solemnly waiting before suddenly, one begins to feel something on the line . . . perhaps a thought is biting! In the evening, I would fall asleep as images of magic lanterns paraded across the backs of my eyelids. Can a life be reduced to this? Yes. But that would be to reduce it to its simplest, perhaps even its most beautiful, expression. The challenge consisted of maintaining this delicate tension.

Between me and the world, there was nothing more than this lukewarm air, several gusts of wind, disheveled patches of grass, and the shadow of an animal. And no screen! No information, no news, no bitterness or anger. My strategy of withdrawal slowly distilled its vitality back into the fibers of my being.

Setting off on the invisible paths, seeking out clearings behind the brambles, was my way of escaping the apparatus society. A pernicious indoctrination was at work within my life as a city dweller: a soft surveillance, a regimentation accepted out of pure laziness. As much as I attempted to ignore them, new technologies invaded every corner of my existence. One shouldn't be hypnotized by them. They're not just ways of simplifying one's life. They slowly begin to substitute themselves for it. They are not a friendly list of mere innovations; they have modified our very existence on earth. It was "brilliant to convince ourselves that we could use them in a fair way," to paraphrase the Italian philosopher Giorgio Agamben in his short manifesto of disgust.[3] These innovations refashioned the human psyche. They took aim at our behaviors. One could already see how they regimented our use of language and served as some form of beta-blockers for our thought. These machines had their own lives. They represented nothing less than a revolution in the life of humanity just as monumental as the birth of the neo-cortex over four million years earlier. Will they improve the species? Render us freer and friendlier? Has life uncovered a bit more grace since it has transitioned its way through the screens? I'm not so sure. It's perhaps even possible to consider that we are actually in the midst of losing control over our existence. For Agamben, we've become "the most docile and cowardly social body that has ever existed in human history." Setting off on the invisible paths implied opening up some sort of breach in the technological ramparts. Containing within myself neither the violence of a saboteur nor the narcissism of an agitator, I preferred simply to flee. Seated on the grass, enveloped in the smoke of a cigarillo, at least I still had the power to forget the screens and hypnotize myself through watching the flight of the vultures above the columbines.

I spent one final night on the plateau before descending toward Moustiers by way of a ravine between two hills. During my descent, I came across a sign indicating to what extent the administrative system still mothered its citizens: *The feasibility of this route is not guaranteed.* Such commentaries should be announced to every newborn baby at the dawn of their life! At Moustiers, under the watch of the Entre-Roches chapel, which clings and is bound to the edge of a cliff, I drank a double shot of espresso and stumbled across a copy of the daily newspaper *La Provence.* Oh, what sadness resides in such titles! And I discover I have massacred sun worshippers in Iraq, that I'm destroying a Greek temple, that I'm spilling tons of oil into the deep blue sea, and that whales churn while leaping in a rather bizarre manner. Humanity lacked its proper clothing. Evolution had given birth to a poorly reared being, and the world was subsequently in almost unbelievable disorder. Moustiers awoke in the morning light in the manner of

Raoul Dufy: leisurely and skimpily clad. If there was one impression to draw from the overall generalized chaos, it was that the local village is less of a dump than the global village.

"Do you have a lighter?" I asked the immaculately dressed gentleman who was seated next to me smoking.

"Can I read your newspaper in exchange?" he bargained.

"You lose," I said. "Violence is winning."

"No," he said, handing me his lighter. "It's not winning."

"Don't you read the newspapers?" I asked.

"Oh, sure, I've read them. But we once actually talked about violence. I've struggled with it. I had a friend who got stabbed in a bar and on the way to the hospital, the bastard got blood all over the seats of my Jaguar!"

September 3, on the Plateau of Valensole

At Puimoisson, I slept in the shade of open-air showers. Nothing encourages a sound sleep more than the subtle flow of water. When I awoke, a nice old woman was helping a man too drunk to walk, perhaps helping him make his way back home. It was a charming vision, a bit Russian in my mind.

I began to gain some ground on my way to the Montagne de Lure via the plateau of Valensole. I walked for hours among well-kept fields, planted with trees and tiled-roof cottages. I bid my farewell to the mysteries of limestone pitches; I would rediscover them again, toward the northwest, on the Montagne de Lure. Between the two mountainous regions, I would have to traverse an immense garden of lavender and somehow attempt to uncover a bit of the joy that still resided somewhere deep inside me. And there was only one solution for such a task: exhaust my inner animal.

On the plateau, in the evenings, the wind would blow, annoyingly, giving off a subtle scent of adventure.

The surrounding hedges and trees provided me with my ration of blackberries, pears, and figs. These vagabond victuals were not difficult to acquire. One merely needed to extend a hand. The fruits were never picked. Beautiful black-and-yellow spiders—*agriopes*—assured their keep. The age when people once gathered to pick wild fruit was over. Or at the very least, the pleasure of such a communal task was no longer so easy to stumble upon while walking on the backcountry paths. And besides, quantities of Chinese jellies brought over in large shipping containers could readily be found in the local grocery. Why risk heading out into the thickets when one could now easily procure what one was seeking right down the street through the import-export business? As my mouth slowly became stained blue from stuffing it full of blueberries, I assured myself that there was some sort of relation between the prodigality of these shrubs and the fall in the price of a barrel of oil to under thirty dollars. Between Valensole and Oraison, at the edge of the Canal de Manosque, I passed by a camp of some other welcome nomads. A couple of women shot me a look with their children by their sides, their hands in their mouths. In the surroundings of the camp, the bushes had been picked clean. The Romani understood quite well the values of such treasures.

I extended my greeting to them and they didn't reply. The Romani remained at the edge of society, and I bore a certain admiration and respect for them. At the beginning of the twenty-first century, certain beings in France could still be found living in a continuous state of emergency. I would certainly not trade anything from my own personal life in exchange for a life of eating nettle soup and living in travel campers. But they bore witness to a particular talent for the art of remaining separate and within their own unique zones of existence. I dared hope that my cross-country walk would at the least afford me the gift of encountering such people: monks, scouts, leftists, impoverished vagabonds, fruit pickers, mushroom hunters, crazy people escaped from the asylum—who knows, perhaps I'd even encounter poets who had taken to engaging in a long walk out in nature. An entire guild capable of moving all by itself instead of inserting itself back into the societal current. Such beings in the midst of walking out in the countryside definitely didn't all belong to the same categories, but they would nevertheless find themselves side by side in their collective movement. Perhaps they all had something to confide to each other and the forest offered an ideal location for such meetings. Geographers gave to such forest crossroads, where the paths converged beneath the foliage, the name "stars." Who would I in fact meet among the stars?

The world suddenly became mauve. Valensole, a plateau of lavender? More like a training ground. The alignment of the rows of lavender had the air of military-like conformity. I had experienced the same feeling in viewing the rigorous order of rubber tree plantations in Malaysia. Here the peasant's paintbrush had produced a perfectly smooth canvas, with long brushstrokes of flat acrylic tints out of which the perspective of profitability was born. The earth had been cemented, washed with chemical products, and domesticated according to the needs of perfumery and the production of honey. The battle against the insects had been won. The reward was nothing more than the inherent silence of a parking lot. Not the slightest hum or buzzing could be detected in the air.

And there I was, wandering in the bluish grooves, clinging to my idiotic Parisian thoughts, somewhat admiring the insects. The cultivators would have no doubt burst out laughing, considering, in spite of the decades spent napalming the land, their ever-present fear of an outbreak of a leafhopper attack on the plants.

September 4, the Durance River, right bank

Was I going to succeed in following the haphazard invisible paths? It was difficult to know since it implied reaching the end of my diagonal line before knowing if I had in fact chosen the proper path. In four hours' time, after walking along the levee of the canals, I would arrive at the town of funerary prayer—Oraison.[4] A dark

Of Ruins and Brambles

place. It's not my fault if a number of names given to urban areas are perfectly suited for puns such as this. Dwellings, warehouses, highways emerged from out of a forest of traffic signs: I had arrived in the kingdom known as the suburbs. Up until now, I had been able to escape this nonplace by hiding in the bushes. Upon my arriving in the town, a series of serious signs and billboards detailed the fate endured by the area over the past several decades: "a city in the countryside." Here, the invisible paths came to a halt. They gave way to the apparatus society. I accepted my defeat and followed the highway into the suburban zone.

The Glorious Thirty had given birth to a new landscape.[5] They had reshaped the cartography of the terrain, reorchestrated the conversation between humankind and the earth. For ten days now, I had snaked my way along streams of asphalt and perceived a certain writing of this recomposition of the terrain. One of the previously inhabited rural areas was completely dead and gone. One could still uncover a memory of it among the ruins of the high plateaus. The shepherds' flocks had been placed in cells in the valleys; the pasture lands, along with the remaining high-altitude routes flooded with hikers, no longer served their function as part of the seasonal transhumance. They were left to the vipers. The high-altitude paths had been all but entirely abandoned. The invisible paths ran through such deserted elevations.

The second rurality was still alive and well. It was hanging on by way of subsidies. How many of these farmers and conventional agricultural workers remained? Half a million? They were solid workers and struggled to continue the ongoing nourishment of the Moloch. The lavender of Valensole, the wheat harvested in Beauce, and the myriad of martyred chickens were the fruits of this technological agricultural production. In the 1960s, European high officials put forth their proclamation that farming and agriculture was nothing more than another industry among others, that raising cattle or producing tires basically followed the same laws of commerce. A common agricultural politics led to the use of chemicals to increase production capacity. In letting the evil geniuses of industry whisper in their ears, the peasant farmers took on a great deal of debt, acquiring even more land and buying even more technologically advanced machines and genetically modified grains. Such developments began to really take off: the price of steak dropped. It was pure chemistry. And it was glorious. And the French president at that time, good ole Giscard, declared France was ready to pave the way of the future. This sort of agriculture was born out of a landscape that was just as artificial as the thousands of miles of paved roads. The fields of hay, thickets, wilderness, swamps, and rising slopes gave way to vast areas of marketable real estate—steppes fenced off with large barns for housing tractors. And then all of a sudden, the prosperity disappeared. Globalization opened up its Frankensteinian market. Shipping containers began hauling around products from all over the world at extraordinarily cheap prices. Brussels suddenly became a less prodigious port. The farmers who had acquired a certain swift increase in both their standard of living and their social status, once again were merely considered to be country bumpkins. And rural areas in France suddenly found themselves like a sick old man lying in bed.

And then we had the third staging of the rural. City dwellers began to gain a certain awareness that a life without inconvenience was worse than a life without radiators and indoor heating. The neorural collectives returned to the countryside after carefully considering the cost of leaving eternity. They took to carefully staging the scene of their return, at the service of the imaginary. Beginning in the 1970s, somewhat urged on by either political disputes, the economic crisis, or the more recent rise of the dematerialization of digital culture, they regained their footing in the fields and headed back out into the hills and mountainous regions; they were the salmon of History. Some of them were content to simply reconstruct a dwelling from out of the ruins. Others sought to welcome the odd passerby for a great communal meal *à l'ancienne* around a table, composed only of their homologous counterparts—the growers of local products. These territories also saw a number of English and Belgians establishing themselves, having grown weary of the onslaught of spitting rains on endless brick walls. They purchased residences on silk farms, repainting the shutters mauve and wondering just how it was possible to prefer the work of Turner to that of Cézanne. I made my way through several areas that perpetuated the museum-like character of the French countryside. Moustiers, Castellane, villages out of brochures that seemed entirely organized by the tourism office. The olive oil merchant was somehow right next to a restaurant called Chez Marius, and groups of motorcycle riders parked their Harleys under the shade of sycamores while they stirred their glasses of fake absinthe (without the wormwood) in front of beautifully restored (but completely empty) churches. This was a kind of "lavender and cicadas" rurality. In Brittany, one would uncover more so a rurality consisting of "galettes and bagpipes." In the Indre-et-Loire, such regional representations of rurality would have led to even more difficulties as such territories required a bit more of a singular personality so the marketers could play off the harmonies of the symbols of the region.

There was yet a fourth face that one could still uncover out in the rural areas. For over fifty years, a kind of reserve army had been growing at the service of poorly treated lands. In the 1960s, a number of pioneering farmers finally stopped viewing farming and agricultural production as open warfare on the landscape and began to refuse implementing the practices of American techniques of using airplanes to chemically alter crops. Instead, they chose to grow and cultivate the land under the appellation of "organic farming," and today their numbers have reached more than seventy thousand. It was easy to laugh at them since what they considered an "innovation" was more a return to much older forms of farming. Or even sometimes, what they considered "traditional farming" used methods that were actually highly technologically enhanced in contrast to their own organic way of farming. In any case, their hearts were in the right place, their fruits were tasty, and their methods had begun to slowly become more and more accepted: today, more than thirty thousand organic farms in France comprise 5 percent of the farmed lands in the country. The specific landscape of organic farming was easy enough to discern: their fields didn't mirror slabs of pavement, nor did their manner of raising livestock resemble prison cells.

I left the town of funerary prayer (Oraison) via a bridge crossing the Durance River and made my way into hills of olive trees toward the village of Lurs, where I would eventually sip a fruit juice on a terrace in the shade of blackberry bushes. The Academy of Medicine had already given me a clear message: no more alcohol. For a great number of years, I had lived a life filled to the brim with memories steeped in vodka. And now: no more! The magic fountain was closed for business. I had certainly collected a rather large debt in the office of excess. No longer allowed to awaken the demons deep inside me, I would have to forgo the grace of the drunkard: a grace of welcoming carnivals into one's skull. And this very evening, under a multicolored sky, ripe for a carafe of wine from Provence, I would simply have to enjoy a flask of water. The landscape was content resembling what it was: below, the Durance flowed. Alongside its banks one could hear the buzzing and humming of an active landscape of striated highways and a myriad of barns. Here, up above, one found a village-museum for readers of Marcel Pagnol. Not one single farmer or peasant could be found. Instead, there was a handful of English dames, walking with their straw hats soaking up the pleasures of the sun. Between these two regions there was a third: empty forests where ivy slowly slunk across the landscape. And here, some sort of invisible path led somewhere. Perhaps it led to a ruin, a stable, or a clearing. That would be a good start. A modest fissure in the present.

I headed down to the ancient twenty-meter-long Roman bridge that led to the entryway of the Ganagobie monastery. In such places, two thousand years earlier, in the shadows of the archway, water nymphs could be heard splashing around. Then the Christian God forced them to seek shelter in caves. It was the same story as the lizards: the eras changed and along with them, new masters were crowned, the lords of the moment withdrew into their hideouts, and new temples were constructed on the foundations of the old ones. Rural forms of existence had also endured such changes. Farmers were forced to change professions. There was no need to be sad about this song and dance. One simply needed to accept bidding farewell and making one's way higher up the mountain slope.

September 5, toward the Mountain of Lure

The night spent at the Ganagobie monastery afforded much-needed rest. The monks had provided me with a cell that was certainly more comfortable than any carpet of dirt I could have constructed. Compline, the final prayer at the end of the day, beneath the vaults of the church, gave off swaths of vaporous contours I imagined must be similar to spiral fumes of opium. I had once tasted the sticky black paste but had never drawn forth its enchanting smoke from a pipe. The surrounding limestone rocks had absorbed these nightly chants since the twelfth century; perhaps it was from these very vibrations alone that the space glowed bright. Men dressed in black preserved their practices and gestures, repeating the same phrases standing upright in the courtyard of the river. Down below in the valley, modern man was full of trepidation. Here, the crew carefully held on to its own expression of anguish. My present admiration transformed into astonishment when I realized that within this celebration born out of strict adherence to the Rule one could see the accumulation of panic-laden sweat for fear of losing one's footing. Why was it that I suddenly had a vision of a shipwreck, of Géricault's *The Raft of the Medusa* flickering before my very eyes? Was I hearing a prayer or some form of imploration? I suspected that these chants of "Please come and help us!" bursting forth under the ancient Roman spires were mere stirrings of the soul. I couldn't help but think that they were a bit incongruous since humans were in no way threatened. In 2050, there will be more than ten billion people residing on this planet. If I had instead heard these same pleas and prayers from the animals in the forest, supplications from the rivers and other waterways, I would have taken them more seriously.

On this fine afternoon, the monks were organizing an interfaith dialogue. They had invited to dinner both a rabbi and the bishop of Algiers. We were seated beneath the blackberry bushes of the esplanade. It was an exquisite hour of the day. The Durance River untangled itself within the golden hues of silt-laden reflections. The rabbi was surrounded by his Pretorian Guard composed of two giant, barrel-chested guys with shaved heads and tailored suits. One could make out Glocks shifting in their holsters as they sat down: in all honesty, the interreligious dialogue had begun quite poorly. And so I left after breakfast, filled with gratitude for the monks' kindness, but gently turning my back on the beauty, eternity, and neurosis.

I had garnered twenty euros at the monastery from an old woman who, after getting one glimpse at my deformed face, had taken pity on me and slipped me the folded paper currency: "You say a mass for whomever you'd like" and I immediately thought of my mother, who would have never asked for such a thing from me. It was the first time my shattered face had elicited such compassion. My accident had led to a partial facial paralysis and my grimace intrigued children I passed on the streets. Even dogs looked at me in a bizarre manner. My contorted mouth sank lower on one side, my nose was rather wonky, my right cheek was sunken in, my eye was bulging. In other words: I was a *freak*. The revived aesthetics of antiquity undertaken by the Renaissance and the classicism of the sixteenth century deeply affected me since they imposed their canons of symmetry. It was only thanks to the deconstruction of cubism in the early twentieth century that we finally had developed some form counter to this imperative of equilibrium. Picasso's paintings consoled guys like me who dealt with partial facial paralysis. The former assured the latter that life could indeed accommodate itself to ugliness. If I had lived during the Middle Ages, smack dab in the middle of Bosch's dreamworld, my disgrace would have gone unnoticed.

I began walking again amid clay-laden ravines speckled with clear ponds and eroded slopes. Creeks sliced their way through the earth, and the roots of green oak trees helped to prevent the loss of soil. As a result of my fall, I had become deaf in one ear and I often lost my balance. Leaning on my trekking poles, I lamented the days when I was still in complete possession of my senses. My sense of smell had also been partially lost, and I could no longer inhale the full breath of Provence, the acrid smell of cistus, or the warmth of the limestone, which served as the smell of light. The sun discharged its vapors within the tree canopy. Cézanne really had no right to have enshrouded his Provence entirely in bluish hues.

· · ·

At the north end of the village of Montlaux, now in ruins perched on a hill of crumbling limestone, Lure Mountain appeared to obscure the horizon. Its shadowy reef of forests barred access to the northern valleys. Before setting my sleeping bag down in a grove of green oaks, I rested on tired legs at the edge of the clearing and spent an hour calmly smoking my boxwood pipe filled with Dutch tobacco. A bell rang out and the late-day church mass of Lure spilled out into the remains of evening. In this year of the twenty-first century, it felt particularly like a good idea to spend an hour doing nothing like a tiny figure in a pastoral painting from the eighteenth century.

September 6

Lure Mountain offered a path toward the countryside of Ventoux. All one had to do was make one's way toward the summit and follow the path of the ridgeline westward.

Reddening beech trees announced my arrival at the summit. The pierced orbitals of the white trunks and the weathered forked branches of the trees lent a resemblance to a decor of the German fantastic. These were forests capable of sheltering creatures from Fuseli, Munch's Madonna, Kubin's nightmares, and Otto Dix's skeletons. I would have certainly been more than eager to contemplate their works while lying on a bed of copper leaves if books of art history weren't so bloody heavy.

Notre-Dame de Lure was a forest chapel built in the shadows of four striking trees on an esplanade at the edge of a dilapidated homestead where Lucien resided. I met him while he was out filling his buckets with water, parting his long locks of hair. It was the perfect place for some sort of chant-fable right out of the eighth century. All that was missing was a battle horse taking in some fresh air and respite alongside a gallant knight drinking a heavy pour of Provençal wine.

"Lucien? They told me about you at the Ganagobie monastery. They say you live here as a hermit?"

"Yes. For a number of years now."

"Is there anything you need?"

"Nothing at all! I have plenty of books. Sometimes they bring me some food rations. Right now, I'm reading a story about some guy who exiled himself in a cabin on Lake Baikal for several months."

"Ah, I know about that guy. He's me."

Lucien was keen to show me a sign he had planted in the ground near the mountain path adjacent to his humble abode: "I accept books and stale loaves of bread."

I still clung to the belief that living like this, separated from all the main traveling routes, in no way guaranteed an ounce of comfort nor any sort of psychological stability, but nevertheless allowed one to escape something much worse: an endless stream of phone calls and waiting in long lines at the grocery store and other shops. In other words: it afforded one a way to undo time and space.

I gifted Lucien my copy of De Quincey's *Confessions of an English Opium Eater* and told him that his motto etched on the sign was a veritable lifestyle brand. Only ten days earlier I had met someone cut from a similar piece of cloth who proclaimed, "Here, we don't have any Wi-Fi connection, but we have plenty of carafes of wine!" These strange places where one still venerated such vital substances would perhaps become temples in a not too distant future. People would flock here in some sort of procession similar to how Japanese pilgrims make their way up into the mountains once a year to kneel in tears at a Taoist altar underneath the blossoming cherry trees.

• • •

I continued on for another three days across the spine of the mountain. Like an old sleeping beast, the shifting paths led me back and forth between the southern and northern side of the Lure. The limestone ground was hard. At times, those who walk in such areas feel as if they are convicts breaking apart their fair share of stones.

Upon arriving at a place called La Fontaine, the fountain, I encountered an old woman who limped gently in front of a loosely assembled stone wall, holding a bucket full of fresh berries. She glanced up toward me, and it was precisely the gaze I was looking for—the cold, hard stare of a peasant, shimmering with ancient forms of knowledge. She belonged to a category of people for whom the health of the growing prunes was vastly more important than internet bandwidth.

"How are things going?" was all I could muster to say.

"There are no more walnuts here," she murmured. "Walnuts have a great appreciation for life, and no one lives here any longer. On the other side [the southern side of the mountain], they still have mushrooms."

"How lucky for them," I said.

"It's a great misfortune! People from the city scurry out here like beetles picking up everything in sight without taking the time to distinguish the edible porcinis from the poisonous toadstools! If they show me their harvests, I don't say a word. They're better off poisoning themselves!"

This old witch was something else! She seemed to fit in well with the other ruins of the Lure. She demolished walls, spoke of old spells, turned worry into a state of mind and manifested the ancient anguish of humanity staring up into the heavens. I made my way back up onto the ridgeline toward Jeambar, and Ventoux suddenly appeared to be getting closer, as if bursting forth and jumping over the Alps, not wanting to die in the south but nevertheless soon collapsing into the plains.

The forest hid these beautiful old Provençal terraced paths—cobbled together with tiny stone embankments called *restanques.* All that effort just to end in ruins! Such terracing of the land indicated how long humans had dwelled at these high elevations, and the herculean tasks they had undertaken to refashion the profile of the landscape for their agricultural benefit. Walking along these sloped, cobbled paths lined with tiny protruding walls, I was practicing a form of living archaeology. It had taken millennia to transform these slopes into an agricultural staircase. And in a matter of decades, these structures had been given over to the undergrowth. Such was the blind force of the era: the speed at which it simply rid itself of old forms.

Moss covered the tiny walls along the path. The brambles were time's subtle caresses of the piles of stone. In its feeble attempts at strangling the walls, a green oak became an impoverished imitation of the trees reclaiming their abode at Angkor Wat.

The results were modest. Why weren't painters interested in depicting such abandoned places? These sites had all the characteristic traits of eighth-century vanitas paintings. Instead of a human skull, an hourglass, and a flower, there was an expanse of stone with an outgrowth of ivy. The symbolic apparatus was slightly different, but the message was the same: everything passes away. The ephemeral nature of the stone wall was even a bit sad since if both man and stone were destined for the same disintegration, the work entailed in edifying the former was certainly more exhausting than reproducing the latter.

September 8, on the edges of Ventoux

When I was occasionally afforded an escape from spending the night surrounded by the four walls of a hostel, I would sleep in the fields. And I soon detected an ever-quickening thinning of my stature. When one loses weight by walking through the landscape, it's a way of leaving a bit of oneself behind on the side of the road. As soon as my eyes would open in the early morning light, the fire deep inside was already stoking itself for the day's movement. These were the moments I perhaps cherished the most in life: quick plunges into obsession.

Ventoux was fast approaching and I would soon be entering the village of Sault. I had chosen to make my way toward Ventoux from the south end of the mountain, where the slopes cut a subtle corner into the landscape, around Comtat Venaissin. These were the last days I'd be spending in the counterscarps of Haute-Provence. I left the citadel, emerged from the shadow zones. Below, one could glimpse the beginnings of the rich and populated alluvial plains. Farther west, I would eventually cross the Rhône River and would then find myself within the Massif Central—"the abandoned countryside," according to the senatorial report. The Comtat was a fertile plain that for centuries had served as the ancient groves and orchards of popes. These lands had now been recently repopulated by new Arab immigrants, British tourists, and Parisian neoruralists. But one could still encounter a number of Provençal farmers, viticulturalists, and local cultivators at the farmers' markets. Upon my arrival in the village of Sault, I contemplated the irony of my situation: having dreamt of the life of a down-and-out, mischievous subject (like my idol, François Villon, boozing it up in local taverns and composing his poetry between two lovers at a hostel), I instead found myself sitting here, drinking a nonalcoholic beverage with a base of almond syrup, taking a break from walking hundreds of kilometers across the countryside and still getting accustomed to the physical maneuvering of my body, like a patient in a sanatorium.

At times like these, I would slowly slink down into a bit of depression, with my eyes half-closed. I was surrounded by a large group of American cyclists. They were around sixty years old, with a tanned and taut beauty of tennis players, their cycling jerseys drenched in sweat. The English language brought them great joy, and they laughed a great deal, displaying their bleached teeth. They yelled at each other from one table across to another and drank cold glasses of rosé, drops of which could be seen falling from the lips of the women among them. They knew how to live and they had no qualms about showing it.

There were entire tourist agencies in Provence that organized such cycling trips, providing the routes and bicycles so that hundreds of cyclists could make their way around Ventoux before returning to spend their evenings in a welcoming gîte. In Tibet, pilgrims also made their way around stupas and sacred mountains in tatters, sporting hallucinated gazes and faces darkened by charcoal smears. In the end, a beggar's pilgrimage and an American's hiking trip were pretty much the same thing: a way to evade boredom. Barbey d'Aurevilly's horrible avowal was our guiding light: "boredom is indeed the god of my life."[6] My current neighbors did a much better job at fighting off neurasthenia than the dandies from Normandy. They partook in a Technicolor Provence, a postcard landscape with tiny villages flanked by ocher-colored mountains.

There was way too much class under this arbor! Suddenly, I was overcome by the creeping feeling that I was not dressed in the proper attire. When an American arrives somewhere nearby, the French always seem to feel as if they resemble some sort of country bumpkin from Normandy in 1944. I got up and quietly departed so as not to disturb these beautiful pink creatures. I had no ill feelings toward them. I didn't think to myself that behind every perfectly manicured smile resided the mask of an ogre. No! Nothing! No sarcasm! Truth be told, I envied their expressions of happiness.

A bit farther along, as night fell, I slept in a clearing of pine trees. A chapel had been constructed there, and so I built a fire at its steps with the immense flourish of the white Ventoux penetrating its way through the tree canopy on the horizon, so magnificent that an unknowing soul may have mistaken it for a giant cloud teaming with shimmering light. This clearing was one of the sites the Christians had taken control of during the time when they built all their chapels in the very same locations where deer had once, for a much longer period of time, also made their summer residences.

September 9, in the region of Comtat Venaissin

Mornings were always the most difficult. I would have to begin by shaking off the bad dreams from the previous evening and then get the old cartilage warmed up. I always found myself returning to the same principle I had borrowed from Napoleon's fleeing grognards or those who had successfully fled the Soviet Union: when one thinks of the most unfortunate person in the world, one slowly begins to console oneself.

As the sun rose above my head, I slowly set off descending into the steep and shadowy, mossy valley below. I came across the tattered ruins of shepherds' quarters at the foot of a series of walls. Up until the Second World War, animals would be stationed here during the periods of transhumance. Evenings within the warmth of the herd were surely profound and adventurous. I regretted a bit not making it to this spot the previous day so that I could have set up my camp here. I also regretted not having arrived here one thousand years earlier.

The hedges shimmered and glistened with light. The spider-webs gave way to my movements cutting through paths, proof that this had once again become virgin territory. I came across stone enclosures one after another. They represented another age when man, spending his time walking through the forest, was not yet someone who prided himself on simply being a *supporter of green spaces.* These vestiges only elevated the solemnity of the shadows. The path opened up onto a perspective. The Comtat slowly deployed itself within the landscape, lined with asphalt. The distant rumbling of motorcycles slowly increased. At my back: the slow organization of pastoral shelters. In front of me: routes and paths zigzagging throughout the valley following the circulation of animals, humans, and merchandise. On this side of the ravine, one could still glimpse the world of the past. Toward the south end resided the present, and already there were signs indicating one's arrival into the suburban areas slowly encroaching on the foothills of Mont Ventoux. The conquest of the French landscape by this new form of habitat had been rather swift. All it had taken was a couple of years after the Second World War for the cosmetic surgery of the geography to commence. In 1945 the country was supposed to collect itself back up and put itself back together. Redrawing the cartography of the landscape was supposed to offer a way to wash away the shame of 1940. A new prosperity would assure the success of the project. The State would shelter the children of the baby boom. Low-rise buildings began to grow at the outskirts of the cities. And then, one slowly began to *pour out the project of urbanism,* as the city planners would call it. Their expression was a logical one since concrete is a sort of liquid. The hour had arrived for an increased opening up of the landscape. The city had begun to gain more ground. It was the era of the ZUP in the 1960s and that of the ZAC in the 1970s. The tentacles of the highway infrastructures began to take hold, and large supermarkets began to appear. The countryside became populated with grain silos. Pompidou was fat and France prospered. Agriculture became industrialized, the number of insects diminished, and the waters became more polluted. Only a few killjoys from Larzac had predicted the encroaching disaster. But they were merely shunned as being leftists, which they were. They were left to reading Lenin in the humidity of their shepherd's quarters.

The celebration of Giscard's seven-year term rang in the second act. A new law concerning urbanism allowed for the construction of homes in agricultural areas. The era of single-family dwellings had begun. Everyone would be able to afford their own paradise on earth. The glorious reveries of abundant lodging shone bright across the entire territory. Seeing it from an airplane, one would have thought that someone had simply turned the sugar bowl over and scattered its cubes throughout the landscape. On the ground one could hear the barking of dogs and the familial home replicated itself to infinity. Children played in the gardens, protected by rows of Thuja. When all was said and done, it was certainly better than the overcrowding of the cityscapes.

Gaston Defferre's decentralization was the true deathblow. Collectivities tend to wash away the keys of their development. "Awake from your sleep, dear countryside!" the State seemed to be blaring. Billboards for big-box supermarkets began to proliferate throughout the landscape, and even the smaller merchants couldn't help themselves. A mammoth's tail brushed aside all the tiny bistros who offered a pastis in the golden hour of the morning to thirsty souls. From then on, if one wanted to drink in the morning, one had to purchase one's quantity at a of big-box shopping center.

Of Ruins and Brambles

Human geography is a form of History. In just forty years the landscape was remolded so cars could flow through it. It had to ensure perpetual movement between dwellings and the parking lots of supermarkets. The country sprouted legions of round-abouts. From then on, humans spent hours every day sitting in automobiles. Geographers speak of the landscape as becoming "pockmarked": a strange, soft tissue belonging neither entirely to the city nor the pastoral countryside, a matrix full of holes be-tween which we circulated in cars.

The internet merely finished the molting transformation by closing the final hatches. After the Glorious Thirty at the end of the twentieth century, we could refer to the first two decades of the twenty-first century as the Clicking Twenty. The first period left its reminders in the landscape: water towers, toll booths, and pylons. The second period has left less of a trace of its effects, merely satisfied with creating a void. The world projected itself onto a screen. We could all just stay home now, surrounded by "neighborhood watch," caring neighbors who were classified as such by all the security signs. On special occasions, a rural era might make an apple tart and organize a card game to revive a bit of energy on a Sunday in one of the more devitalized villages. "Personalized service" had replaced our old notions of friendship and video surveillance guaranteed the proper ambience.

In the beginning, things had to have been rather exciting. Our parents surely remember those times: skirts began to shorten, surgeons started to reap the rewards of medical innovation, the Concorde could connect one to America within a few hours, and in the end, Soviet missiles were never actually launched—it was the good life! From out of the lottery of History, the children of 1945 had really struck gold living during those prosperous years. They certainly had not paid heed to Jean Cocteau's speech to the youth of the year 2000: "It is quite possible that Progress is the development of an error."

But the thin pages of maps depicting the landscape at 1:25,000 scale were a precious security blanket. They shared their invisible paths so one could snake one's way through the dead coral reefs. What's important in life is to equip oneself with a good pair of blinders.

· · ·

A local farmer and cherry juice vendor installed his trailer at the edge of Bédoin and I bought two liters, which I gulped down way too fast.

"Do you still see shepherds around these parts leading the transhumance on foot?" I asked.

"You're joking, right? The shepherds are bourgeois now! They head up there in pickup trucks and have TVs in their cabins!"

Above Bédoin, I climbed the stony mountainside toward the Col de la Madeleine. A burning silence could be heard rising from the ground. One of those moments when even the insects remain silent . . .

I continued onward thanks to the shade, blackberries, a bit of a cool breeze, and air-conditioned memories.

At the so-called Combe Obscure, memories from my journeys here from twenty years earlier slowly began to surface. At that time, I had come to climb the limestone cliffs surrounding the path high above the oaks. A soldier in camouflage pants was making his descent as fast as lightning down the path.

"You getting some good climbs in?" I asked.

"Yeah, up there!"

He made a vague gesture above and had a somewhat timid accent.

"Foreign Legion?" I asked.

"Yeah."

"Where are you from?"

"Latvia."

He continued on his way and ten minutes later the rest of the group unfurled and spilled out in front of me all in a row. A number of Asian individuals, some bright-eyed fellows, some with buzz-cuts, others were rather big fellows who hailed from some islands or other. Legionnaires—men of the world.

I headed on toward Malaucène, untangling the stone paths in the forests, and climbed my way back up toward the Col de la Chaîne. The forest filtered the sunlight like a great woven tapestry, and I traversed the interspersed rays as if each time I washed my face with every explosion of clarity.

My body began to give way a bit. Forty kilometers was too much for a skeleton. Provence had been a somewhat cruel chaperone. What did all this have to do with the Azurian representations I spoke of just a while ago that the Americans sought by way of the handlebars of their bicycles? If they had read the work of Jean Giono, they would have never journeyed here in the first place. The area did not exactly adhere to the images depicted in *To Catch a Thief*. Alfred Hitchcock had composed a perfect marketing diaporama of nestled villages. As for the novelist from Manosque, Giono's pen spit back up the very venom of the landscape. His Provence howled in the stark winds and moaned underfoot. Stones flourished here; they hardened the landscape. Water was a rare resource and nature was a cannibal. The climate offered storms or heatwaves to a vegetation made of thorns. Animals devoured each other, with protruding jaws. Provence? More like a bear.

. . .

That night, on the southwest face of Ventoux, centipedes visited me in my dreams. Already beginning during my nights spent at Lure I had received a number of bites at the crease of my elbows. I could hear a myriad of creatures rustling about in the darkness. Boar and foxes patrolled the surroundings. Then, all of a sudden, there was a ballet of helicopters. The apparatuses from the Orange hunting club had begun their nocturnal training. They cut quickly around the cols like a sharp razors and worked on stationary hovering before plunging toward the other side of the mountain close to Malaucène. Were they Tigers? Fennecs? I had trouble recognizing models based solely on the sound of the turbines. With their detection systems, however, I have no doubt that they could see my body stretched out on the ground. But a guy sleeping outside under the light of a half-moon was clearly of no concern for a helicopter doing training exercises.

September 10, at Séguret

With the helicopters now departed, the animals resumed their more discrete paths. Certain of them would try to bring back a bit of order to the chaos of the Orient. Others would try to hole up in a specific territory where man, dressed in some sort of hat, would tolerate them so they could occasionally still go out and attempt filling them with a bit of buckshot.

The vultures were already on the lookout, high up in the white sky as I set about walking again in the morning light. I had slept well, like a rock, and after only one hour of a joyous hike, coming to a spine in the limestone, I had reached an inlet: "le Pas du Loup." The blackberries were slowing down my average mileage. I had to stop at every bush to pick them. Such gluttony led to my hands bleeding. The risk of scratching oneself for the pleasure of fruit brought something else to mind: a love story. At the very threshold of a day of seasonal fires, with no other imperative than to merely continue onward a bit. Without anyone to get hold of, without anyone to have to respond to. A day outside, a day sheltered from it all.

At the foothills of the Cheval Long, I suddenly began to catch a glimpse of the rows of industrialized grape vines sprayed with copper sulfate. The earth between the plants was a uniform surface. The weeds had been plucked out: they resembled the steppe after Genghis Khan's troops had made their way through. Every grape seemed to resemble the next, plump and crammed full of chemical doping agents. Sometimes one could still find plots where wild grasses grew in a less regimented manner: these were referred to as organic—without the additional administering of chemical additives or treatments. They provided a wine that was easier on the connoisseur's conscience. A wine one could drink without worrying about the grandchildren.

Farther down, having passed by Rasteau, I traversed the great muddy plains, the alluvial folds of the Rhône offered to man by God in order for any true Frenchman to get hammered on a real glass of red.

In the distance, the village of Séguret slowly turned into a sharp sliver of limestone, like a douar in the Atlas Mountains. An ideal post for keeping watch over the enemy. Yesterday it was the invaders of the tenth century or the Huguenots. Tomorrow? Who knows? Séguret occupied high elevation at the folds of the pre-Alpine landscape. The fruit-bearing plains of the Comtat had begun. Sablet, at the foot of the butte, was already an agricultural barrier, nothing more than a collective of farm properties rather than a protective fort. Trickling brooks of water surged forth as if by contact. Adjacent to this "source of fairies," a snake[7] sought a bit of humidity. It slithered off as I arrived, slowly at first, since its belly clung to and scraped itself on the path; then it shot off into the tall grass once it had freed itself from the erosion.

The young oak trees all bore signs to discourage plunderers: "No truffle hunting allowed." Since Mercantour, I had been amazed at man's propensity to posterize his injunctions. Every border bore its own version of "No poachers," "No hunting allowed," "Private property," "No trespassing," and I even saw one sign that said, "Final warning." Humans certainly knew how to manage nature, to fence it off, to *anthroposize it,* as the geographers would say. Evolution was a strange thing. In just thirty thousand years, it had gone from a group of hunter-gatherers to slowly multiply and conform humanity's reflexes into that of tiny property owners.

In Séguret, I slept at the home of a dear aunt who welcomed me like a mother. For a long time, she had lived amid the wind currents of various islands and had acquired from those years an art of living under pergolas. Hers opened up onto the plains at the foot of some large rocks where the winding curves of the Rhône could be seen, fifty kilometers in the distance, changing its hues under the rays of the sun. Toward the west, beyond the river, a storm grumbled above the Cévennes. The next eminence to overcome. And for the moment, I took the grumblings as a bad omen.

September 14, toward the Rhône

We were smack dab in the middle of the grape harvest. Amid the heat, the madness of the earth seeped through its pores. The vines would soon give back in splendor and contentment what they had plucked from the sunlight. A group of Spaniards were busy, spread out in various rows: a veritable red brigade. A worker could be seen, clad in boots, smoking at the edge of a path that had been drenched by the storms from the previous day.

"¡Hola! Is it gonna be a good harvest this year?" I asked.

"I foresee good money!" he replied, smiling.

At the beginning of the afternoon, I settled into a siesta with my neck on my backpack to avoid the mud, leaning against the vines. And I awoke thinking to myself that I somehow probably reflected what some would consider the perfect image of France: a guy snoring at the foot of a grape vine. Perched on the high hills of the Aigues, on the ancient castrum of Cairanne, I left for Sérignan, twenty kilometers to the south. Jean-Henri Fabre settled there in 1889. A naturalist (he didn't like the label *entomologist*), he isolated himself in a garden there where he acclimated tropical species, rare trees, and baroque insects. He regaled himself on the *harmas,* the Provençal term for wilderness, and its cabinet of curiosities, aligning shells, pinning down butterflies, and setting himself to his studies. For three decades he collected plants, ran up and down the foothills of Ventoux, studied the evolution of species, collected fossils, adored animals, and composed unforgettable "entomological memories" on a small wooden table. Reading them taught me that we could open ourselves to the world within the secret machinations of a garden. One could forge a system of thought simply by closely eyeing various out-growths of vegetation, while leaving aside the protected prosper-ity of certain grumblings about the world and instead develop a totalizing philosophy that in no way propelled humanity to the center and summit of every contemplation. Worthy of the noblest art or jeweler's craft, an insect is a key for unlocking the mysteries of the living.

My heart was certainly closely aligned with such thinkers. They had dedicated their lives to remaining in the shadows of ce-dars. At times, they would even consent to climbing up a moun-tain merely to capture a beetle. And the rest of the time, they pretty much stayed home, reminding us that too many trips around the world were a rather vain endeavor. Why should one spend one's entire life endlessly cavorting around? What does one bring back from all these adventures? A bunch of memories and a lot of dust. The traveler accumulates experiences and uses up a great deal of energy. He returns out of breath muttering, "I'm free," and then hops right back on another airplane. Since my fall, I have been more tempted by *harmas*.

Two thousand one hundred years ago, before the mad one of the bush, a Greek had revealed that the art of governance was per-haps not that dissimilar to running a farm. Xenophon had turned his *Oeconomicus* into a manual for commanding masquerading as a handbook on agronomy. You want a bit of power? All you need to do is cultivate a bit of land! At six o'clock in the evening I sat on the slope overlooking Aigues and stared out into the valley. Structures built in the eighteenth century were shrouded beneath a checker-board of vines. The cypress stood guard in front of the stone walls.

The proprietors of such grounds held a much more effec-tive power than any president of the French Republic. The for-mer presided over a very determined and concrete fate of a small kingdom. The latter, being responsible for the masses, tossed out abstract wishes intended to orient the course of a machine much more powerful than he: History. The power of a president largely consisted of weaving in and out of a labyrinth of mishaps and interdictions.

A landowner could pretty much defend his forest however he wished from attacks by any kind of xylophage. A head of state often faced criticism for his or her tactics considered to be extreme when the country was threatened.

In terms of governance, the modesty of one's ambition better assured its accomplishment. The limit of the exercising of power guaranteed its efficiency. And efficiency was the substance of power. "I don't want to know anything about my powerlessness," the president would say. "My land is my kingdom," replied the property owner. "I want what I can't have," moaned the head of the executive branch. "I'm only capable of what I know," whispered the master of places.

And while one of them took to overseeing his harvest and his animals, the other one was under the illusion of ruling over the inaccessible, of having an influence on the irrepressible.

Recently, the presiding French president decided to take a crack at changing the current protocols and strategies concerning global climate change when he wasn't even capable of protecting his own butterflies and bees (which would certainly have brought tears to Fabre's eyes).

Like demented kings from German fairy tales, sporting hats with bells, manipulated by magicians, the global heads of state wander inside their palace walls, convinced that the agitated whirling of their arms will lead to a complete architectural overhaul of hyperatrophied societies whose decisions were based on calculations and maintained by virtue of renouncements. State politics was an art of the expression of one's intentions. The *Oeconomicus* of the agricultural domain was that of realizing ideas within a reduced space. This was Xenophon's lesson and contribution.

Owning no land, I merely attempted to be sovereign over myself by walking on the paths. I avoided asphalt. I sometimes slept outside. That was pretty much all I could control.

I set out again toward Mondragon, where I arrived as night fell over the valley of the Rhône.

The small hotel where I collapsed for the evening was crammed full of grape harvesters. We all ate dinner in the common area in front of the television. One of the advantages of having lost the ability to hear in one of my ears was that the sound was already lowered. I had no idea what the woman on channel BFM was saying: she seemed panicked by the idea of simply letting something happen. In my bag I had a copy of Fernand Braudel's *L'identité de la France* and I read the introduction while I lapped up my soup. According to the historian, France was the result of an "extraordinary fragmentation" of peoples and landscape. Braudel considered the country an anomaly. To have pistou eaters living next to Cambrai lacemakers in the same territory (and under the same flag) was an utter miracle. Grace had allowed for the coexistence of contrasting physiques and their psychocultural incarnations: limestone and granite, seals and scorpions, Protestants and Catholics, tiny Savoyards and shepherds from the Landes, the royalist Charles Maurras alongside the socialist Jean Jaurés. The normal fate of such contrasts was civil war. And yet two thousand years of rumblings had eventually been reabsorbed into a unity (of course, at the cost of some discord). A certain temptation appeared to seduce contemporary governing bodies to choose what they preferred the most in the boutique of History: "the right to inventory," using the expression and language of someone stocking shelves in a store.

Good ole Fabre, whose lands I had just made my way through, had come up with a different expression to add to Braudel's meditations. He described the earth's various fossil layers as a *pâte des morts*—a "dough of the dead." We have lived on top of a compression of billions of dead microscopic organisms digested by time and whose stratification has composed a substratum. The so-called impossible France was like limestone: arising out of a great digestion. The slowly unfolding rumination of contrary ideas, contrasting climates, irreconcilable landscapes, and dissimilar peoples had eventually kneaded a viable dough. For Braudel, that's where identity resided: inside an *amalgam,* a splendid term. It had taken dozens of centuries.

My evening ended up being horrible. The idea of a diffracted country—while also being unified—prevented me from getting a good night's sleep. The name of my place of lodging might as well have been called "Roy's Rest Stop."[8] The rumble of the long-haul trucks shook the cardboard walls of my thirty-euro-a-night hotel room next to the national highway.

September 15, below the Île Vieille

A day amid puddles. The arrival of daybreak brought with it humidity, and as I headed toward the Rhône each of my steps seemed to stick in the mud. On the alluvion folds of the Île Vielle that separated me from the Rhône, I passed alongside reed beds from which no creature took flight. Not a swish or a bird chirp. The vegetal feathers swayed back and forth in the easterly wind with the grace of a metronome. I passed through orchards where the grape harvesters were still hard at work. I thought of the "dough" of France. At the very place where I was walking, in just a smattering of centuries, hunters from the Magdalenian age, Hannibal's elephants slowly journeying toward Rome, Huguenots after Provençal blood, and a whole procession of rural ancestors— soldiers of the Empire or simply common vacationers, pedaling their bicycles on the national highway 7. Today, the asphalt roads followed alongside the river, TGV speed trains, and the A7 highway. Joggers sporting headphones waved at me, and I could slowly make out the panache of the billowing smoke from the nuclear Installations at Pierrelatte. A nuclear power generator, a memory of

Of Ruins and Brambles   **53**

Hannibal: This was what could be described as a Braudelian accumulation—a compression of images concerning the same acre of land. To quote the wise old owl Peter Sloterdijk, who always gives the impression of being wrested from sleep by his own thoughts, "Space was invented so that we aren't all in the same place." He could have said the same thing about time. Time wasn't as compact as Fabre's "dough of the dead." The succession of events doesn't leave impressions as easily mixed together as a fossil in a layer of limestone. One had to try to perceive the vestiges of the past by searching through the layers of the ground, by gazing out at the landscape, and scrutinizing certain faces.

The invisible paths whose threads I was weaving bore this great responsibility of sketching a cartography of a lost time. They had been abandoned because they were already too ancient. This practice was no longer considered a virtue.

3

THE INVISIBLE PATHS

IN THE REGION OF ARDÈCHES

September 16, close to le Bas-Vivarais

Nourished by the recent storms, the Rhône had overflowed its banks. I crossed the river at Pont-Saint-Esprit, glancing at the rapids downstream. How in the bloody hell did all those elephants traverse these currents? They had wrenched these poor elephants away from their quiet meditations on the savannah to set them off on a road to take down Caesar. What in the heck does a pachyderm, lost in the depths of its own melancholy, have to do with the fate of an empire? I made one final jaunt out onto the twelfth-century bridge so as to turn around a final time and glance back in the direction of Ventoux, as if to hold on to and engrain an image of the mountain in my memory. I did not want to forget that geology had constructed its altars high above the plains, long before man began to imitate it with his large bell towers underneath which he attempted to convince himself that a God external to his own creation had had a go at its own geotectonics.

On the other side, the right bank, I set out following the course of the Ardèche River. The rise in the water level had given the river a caramel color. For two days I chose to walk close to the rocky ridge of the gorges or in the forest on the right bank toward Vallon-Pont-d'Arc. On the very first night, a deluge came thundering down. Showers are usually rather brief south of the Loire but

these particular storms kept on pummeling the landscape throughout the night and into the next day. The forest had become somber.
The trees were like bent spines wringing themselves out. I thought
of all the animals without land, wandering through the water run-
off in the Laval woods. And more specifically, I first took care to
seek out shelter for myself in some old, dilapidated forest cottage
before then extending my thoughts toward them—one shouldn't
get carried away and exaggerate one's notion of compassion. The
rain simply wasn't stopping. I left and headed toward a hostel in
Labastide-de-Virac when night finally decided to fall on the forest.

September 17, in the Païolive Wood

The next several days consisted of me trying to carve out an invisible path as much as I possibly could. This region was less populated and so the exercise proved to be a bit easier. At night I would
calculate how much time I had been able to stick to following a
network of forgotten paths. I would sometimes revel in the satisfaction of having covered three-quarters of the estimated number of kilometers. In eyeing Les Vans, I headed in the direction of
Mont Lozère. The rains had overtaken the bridge at the stream of
Lantouse, near Vallon-Pont-d'Arc, and I began to recall the question we often had to ask ourselves when we were traveling in Ne-
pal and were confronted with bridges that had been ripped away
by frothing rivers: are we going to have to suffer through an extra
four days of hiking simply to get to the other side? Here, such in-
conveniences in the geography of France meant lengthening one's
route only by an additional handful of kilometers. Such was the
advantage of residing in small countries that had been well managed and planned like Japanese gardens. I stayed on the left bank,
and in the wooded areas of shrub oak high above, on a stone path,
I encountered two old, very chic-looking Austrians resembling
Stefan and Lotte Zweig on a walk before their suicides, him wearing a tweed blazer and her a cream silk scarf. They were carrying

wood in a wheelbarrow. Even the logs were neatly arranged. Their ruin, a perfectly restored structure, could be seen above in the distance, its roof sporting Roman tiles.

"After the evacuation," he said (I'm presuming he was referring to the rural exodus), "everyone came here to buy a farm: the Belgians, the English . . . and us."

With a thin pointed finger, he quickly showed me a shortcut I could take to the Col de Cize through the oak grove, and I trudged my way the rest of the day above slabs of limestone referred to as "serres" in the Ardèches region. The abandoned hamlet of Chastelas took up part of the slope above the farmed plains. Undergrowth had slowly dismantled the lintels and created a fissure between the remaining masonry that was still intact.

In such villages, I lived several hours of perfection. At the fountain in the shadow of a linden tree, on a bench leaning against the back wall of a church: all the necessary elements for a rest break in the manner in which Hesse or Hamsun furnished them for the characters in their poetic promenades. On the path of the Plateau of Païolive, where the silt gently clung to each of one's steps, I encountered one such character: an old man in camo cargo pants and a khaki hat. It was precisely the silhouette I had been seeking! A guy carving out his own paths in the countryside. A thin and free shadow on an invisible path!

"You look like Fidel Castro walking through and inspecting the tobacco fields," I exuberantly proclaimed.

"Minus the cigar," he replied.

"No, but you certainly have the right hat, and then there's that!" I pointed at the crops that I couldn't recognize but that certainly wouldn't have gone unidentified in Cuba.

"Sorghum! When I returned from the factories, they had already begun growing these new crops. During the war, we secretly grew tobacco."

"You should take out the sorghum and grow tobacco again!" I exclaimed.

"Good idea!"

He bid me a "farewell!" and set off again with his own enthusiastic rhythmic strides creating a suction noise after every step across the mud. And I continued with my little steps, because I was afraid of slipping and it was the golden hour of the evening when the bones in my back began pleading for grace and a respite. I knew how to politely ask them for one or two more hours before the evening pause. At this moment in the day, the same thought would creep into my heart. It was a painful and powerful punch: "Twenty years of climbing up ridgelines to arrive here, moving at the pace of an old woman." I referred to my inconvenience as *the irony of sports*.

I turned around to watch the path maker continue his progress downstream on the brook. The old bastard was making quick work of it! With all due respect to Charles Mauras, champion of the notion of the *true land* in contrast to the *legal land*, walking on the invisible paths allowed one to discover a land that was at the same time *illegal* and *irreal*. Illegal because we could sleep at the foot of a campfire that was deemed forbidden and because you would certainly come across bizarre folks of all types: wanderers, Romani, a couple of local knucklehead farmers or country bumpkins, some cantankerous individuals who were still a bit rough around the edges, savages employing a singular vocabulary who accepted listening to pretty much anything and everything. Irreal because you would often encounter ghosts as well.

On this fine evening, the ghosts rested in the Païolive Wood, where I had arrived by way of a karstic plateau thick with clouds of gnats forming a cumulus of proteins above the grass. A chaos of limestone blocks populated the forest above the Chassezac, whose currents flowed between two cliffs eaten away by caves. Five-meter-high blocks formed a kind of protective layer for the woods. And the sun made the rocks glisten. A spirit who had a predilection for daydreaming would have thought the approaching herd of people were petrified, but they were simply grabbing hold of the cliff edge in order to throw themselves back off it.

"Stop dreaming, Tesson. Night is falling."

Cédric Gras had joined up with me on my adventure the day before in the village of Vallon-Pont-d'Arc, and we had walked down this path all day long in silence. I had known him for ten years. I read his books and he accepted my preferences for swearing in Russian, strong alcohol, and complicated evenings often as a result of these two predilections. He had worked these past ten years in Russia, which we both considered a second homeland due to its geography and a couple of its inhabitants. We had got lost together in the middle of the Russian forests of the Far East, and we had drunk beer together sitting in the Donetsk city hall protected by some Russophone separatists, and we had also made a couple of successful improvised mountain climbs. Gras had never once made any antagonizing comments about my amateur-ish mountain-climbing skills since he himself had fractured his leg at six thousand meters in the Karakorum and was still alive thanks to the dual effort of an Italian climbing rope and a Pakistani helicopter pilot. His conception of human relations was to never compare the value of a feeling to the frequency of its expression.

• • •

That evening we made a fire on the edge of a cliff above the Chassagnes. Birds of prey cut through the air. Throughout the dark of night, the wind continually played chimes with our tents, echoing a specific clanking sound, like the one that passes through a ship's sails, waking dozing sailors from their slumber every fifteen minutes or so. At midnight, Gras, as regimented as a bat, began to speak.

"You know, we've traveled, traversed, and run around the whole world, and we still don't understand a single thing about all this chaos."

"The walker is not worthy of what he treads upon," I replied.

"There's a scene in Tolstoy's *Cossacks* where the old soldier takes the young soldiers out into the forest right after they have graduated and completed their training in military school. They are all brilliant officers. They have their diplomas, they have their science, their medals, but they can't pick out the tracks made by the animals on the ground. They can't decipher the signs of the wind blowing through the trees. And the old soldier says, 'They're all knowledgeable, but they don't know anything!'"

"That's us," I said.

"Man, you know, Tesson, the rurality you keep going on about is a life principle established on immobility. If someone is rural it's because they remain within the unity of a place from which they welcome the world. They don't leave their land. The framework of your life can be delineated simply by walking and captured through your eyes alone. You are fed off what grows within the length of your action. You don't know anything about Korean cinema, you don't give a shit about the American primaries. But you know why a certain kind of mushroom grows precisely at the end of this layer of soil. From out of a fragmented knowledge, one eventually arrives at the universal."

"The universal is the local minus the walls." I replied. "You ever heard that saying by Miguel Torga?"

"No," he said. "We, we are modern."

"We move on to other things."

And we eventually even ended up falling asleep.

September 18, in the Vivarais region of the Cévennes

We were seeking out the invisible paths. We headed onto the trails where plates of rock blessed by the sun flourished, and we drank rainwater from limestone basins. We lusted after undergrowth. One had to pay attention and not miss where the next trail began. Often, the sun gleamed off a rock, and we sat in its glistening reflection like cats playing, offering ourselves up to the light and stretching our muscles.

Gras walked fast and I struggled to keep up. But each day led to an improvement in my physical functioning. At times, I could get a sense that my flexibility was returning. Other times, I felt less short of breath. And today, I hadn't felt one single ache or pain in my back. For the moment, my healing led me to a kind of unnatural feeling: as if the demolition of the biological process of life had been inverted and I was going to regain my youth until the day when, having healed, the machinery would invert itself again and I would start to feel I was growing old again. A sign that I had completely recovered.

We were dying of thirst, and upon arrival at an empty farm we raised the cover of a well and disturbed a proud black scorpion. Perfectly armored, with his well-equipped pincers—a tiny god. His superpower? He knew exactly what he was doing. He disappeared within the shadows of the well. Was it the fractures of my skull that had bestowed upon me a strange acuity for detecting arachnids? No doctors had mentioned anything about acquiring such abilities as a result of shocks to the brain. Since my fall, I seem to notice more Reduviidae and centipedes. Not to mention bats. Up until then, as a faithful reader of Lovecraft and Romanticism, I had always considered them as creatures found in nightmares. For the moment, I no longer seemed to be afraid of them and had even taken to loving them. They lived in ruins. They remained in the shadows. They were the sentinels of the places I was seeking out. Pincers forward and jaws at the ready: the paladins of the invisible paths.

We walked with our ears perked. It was hard to avoid hearing all the rumbling coming from the roads. A new time had displaced man and had given him the injunction of circulating and this movement constituted the primary organizing trait of societies. In the global village, everyone awaited their turn at the accordion waltz in the perpetual shuffle. The dam had been opened and the currents had increased, and we were merely the silt of an overflowing river. Overflowing its banks, feeding itself on more and more mobile materials and whereby each element appeared to be replaceable by another. Who, I wondered, would be the one to dam up the Amazon?

Historians had invented various expressions for naming the ages of humanity: the Stone Age, the Iron Age, the Bronze Age was overcome and then there was the feudal age and those of antiquity. These forms of time were immobile. Our current age suddenly gave way to the "flux age." Airplanes traversed the planet, cargo drifted, and particles of plastic floated in the oceans. Even your average everyday toothbrush had more than likely traveled around the world. This vertiginous movement had even become a kind of dogma. A culture had to give itself over to circulation and contacts if it wanted a chance of seeing itself celebrated. The ode to "diversity," "exchange," and the "communication of universes" was the new catechism of professionals and cultural production in Europe.

The Parkinson's disease of History was called globalization. The translation of this phenomena in our daily lives implied being able to find tropical fruits and vegetables in the most remote and modest country supermarket. A question then came to mind: Why was it that we wouldn't allow someone to steal an apple from an orchard, but we were completely fine with allowing a Brazilian mango to hold court in a grocery store in the Ardèche? Where did the true infraction begin?

As the planet was promised a theater of a general circulation of beings and products, in contrast, the valleys were afflicted with their large highways and the mountains with their tunnels. The "management of territory" also organized movement. Even the blue hues of the sky above our heads were striated with a panache of long-haul aircraft. The very landscape itself had become the mere scenery of passage.

Rurality, in principle, established itself as a resistance to this general impulse. By choosing to be sedentary, one created an island within the perpetual flow. In plunging onto the invisible paths one navigated from one island to the next. For over a month now, I had fought my way through this archipelago.

In the village of Vans, the waiter behind the bar served up the same typical question. My response was always the same: "From Mercantour . . . and I'm going to go as far as I can . . . toward the English Channel . . . perhaps." The young man made a comment that piqued the interest of Gras's geographical spirit: "If your walk goes well today, you'll sleep on top of granite tonight."

And the soda merchant was in fact correct! The sudden change in universes took place around Brahic, at 600 meters of altitude. The houses made of granite were covered with roofs of stone slate. The chestnut trees were stationed at the border, indicating the change in the landscape. The Provençal coats of arms—limestone, olive trees, and Roman tiles—were finished. From here on out, we were changing heraldry. To the east, we left behind us the spirit of the air traversed through the sun: Provence. Here, on the slopes of a gigantic volcanic massif, the spirit of a very old fire slept under the chestnut burs.

As we climbed up into forests, one could hear the squealing of the leaves of the chestnut trees underneath our feet. The savoring of the days would not be the same as the shore of granite we had just passed through. I knew I was being influenced by geology. Limestone, slate, and lava dictated my moods. Certain people firmly hold to this principle whereas others do not. "Not a single thing in common do we have, the earth and I," claimed Lamartine in his poem "Isolation."[1] Oh how the soul can be so wrong! This word was from a poet in his ascot. It was quite normal that a Romantic poet untethered from his mountain would elevate the *idea of nature* above nature itself. Beneath the chestnut trees I realized just how wrong Lamartine truly was. The air was charged with a new acridness; it pierced right through to the marrow of my bones.

The ridgeline of the Serre de Barre shot out directly westward. We headed in a direction of 270 degrees on a forest service road. Then we connected back up with the invisible paths in the closely cropped thickets, losing a bit of altitude. At times, we had to acquiesce, weaving various links in the invisible paths across some slabs of tarmac. This was admitting a bit of defeat on my part, proof that I hadn't succeeded in sticking to my lines of flight, either because there was no path to follow or because I had given in to fatigue and sought out the easiest path possible. In the forest overlooking the village of Villefort, we slept close to a small fire that joyously shined bright over an evening that had been, in my estimations, a bit too brief. I stared into the flames as if I had won a match against the enchanting spells of the fire gods: any sense of a headache while blowing into the embers of the fire had all but vanished by now.

September 19, toward Mont Lozère

The hills continued on one after the other. Mont Lozère was in our sights. We were entering a territory where cattle herders battled it out against the bush. To use the language of the countryside, this was referred to as "opening up the landscape." Like the Mongolian steppe or the Mattoral shrubland, the high prairies of Lozère were the result of this patient rage practiced by domesticated animals chomping away at the vegetation. The herds seemed insatiable and tireless, but every generation never seemed to forget that the shrublands and undergrowth were like a sea swell. If the animals recoiled and turned back, the undergrowth of the wilderness would return. In France, since the 1970s, millions of anarchic hectares have grown back and reclaimed the land: the stuff from which invisible paths were created.

In the woods overlooking Cubières, we crossed paths with four hunters, guns resting on their shoulders. They each weighed in at around 220 pounds and one of them had three chins. Killing animals that were better toned than oneself didn't help resolve matters of one's portly stature.

"You guys should really be wearing some brightly colored clothes to avoid any accidents," exclaimed the first one in the group.

In other words, they were basically reprimanding us, which really pissed off Gras.

"My good sirs," he replied, employing a tactic he had acquired in Russia of using a more refined manner of talking when confronted with brutes. "We are confused to have to force you to exercise your sense of observation."

"That's a bit ironic, don't you think?" the guy replied.

"We have no other weapons at our disposal," replied Gras.

. . .

One day when we were navigating across the Bikin River, north of Vladivostok, I heard Gras hurl a rather interesting phrase at a group of Russians who were insulting him with the epithet *motherfucking cocksucker*. Gras's refined response: "Good sirs, I'll have to ask you to please refrain from cursing." Which the whole group of guys immediately stomached like a whip across the face.

September 20, near Gévaudan

A trail began to gain in altitude on the north side of Mont Lozère. The trail was called Route des Chômeurs—*route of the unemployed*—and had been constructed in 1936. We both agreed that this name was to our liking and had a rather soviet character to its appellation.

"Even we, the French, were capable of great collective efforts!" Gras exclaimed.

On the ridgeline of the mountain, in fierce winds, we took measured strides and cut our way through the anemic grasses. It was the proper atmosphere for walking. But geography never remains static in the way we'd like it to, save for on the Russian plains, where a uniformity seals one's need for order. We were prepared to walk endlessly as long as the trail followed the ridgeline.

Mont Lozère would eventually collapse, however, and we would have to redescend and leave the dorsal border separating the Protestant south from the Catholic territories.

Over the next two days, we traversed high limestone plateaus with a smattering of ruins that swept across the landscape. One should have pity for such remnants—or perhaps one should envy them? We made our way cautiously without worrying about anything other than maintaining a path and our impatient taste for the fruits that would offer themselves up to our gaze during our movement: a hazel tree, the flight of a grebe, a barn with drystone walls. That was all we needed to be satisfied. We had somehow extracted ourselves from the apparatus.

The apparatus was the sum total of the various behavioral heritages, social solicitations, political influences, and economic constraints that determined our fates without making itself felt. The apparatus managed us. It insidiously and sneakily imposed a certain behavior on us without our ever noticing an increase in its power. There is a tiny worm, a parasite, that infects ants and controls their movements to keep them immobile on a blade of grass. The ants then offer themselves up to herbivores, whereby the parasite finds a new host. The tiny worm was the apparatus for the ant. Silicon chips were our apparatus worms. Each one of us carried our own parasite, with all one's might, in the guise of one of these microprocessors that regulated our lives. The Papuan people transmitted a worldview from one generation to the next containing the idea that the spirit world intervened in the realm of reality. That was how their apparatus functioned. Our apparatus pursued our comfort, our health, and our alimentary opulence, but in doing so also inculcated us with its discourse and kept a good eye on us. We received its information, its advertising, and we responded to its demands. It overwhelmed us with its summarizations, diluted within the brouhaha of life. Even the discourse of the apparatus was an apparatus. On the invisible paths, we plunged ourselves into silence and we exited the apparatus. The first forest that presented itself served as a means of escape. The nightly news here was rather charming, almost undetectable, and difficult to harvest: a barn owl had made a nest in the framework of a mill, a falcon was wreaking havoc on the headquarters of some sort of rodent, a slow worm was dancing among the roots. Stuff like that. They had some importance as well. And the apparatus pretty much ignored all of it.

Upon our arrival in villages, we would take a quick nap, close to the fountains where one could see public notices indicating "noninspected water." We had crossed through ravines of blue marl that had been ravaged by rainfall and stumbled across valleys full of lakes where families picnicked. The paths languished in their undulations. We spent the night on a wooded slope that overlooked the Mende, and the next morning it was all the more special to know that, in hearing the village awake, we had escaped its rumblings for another night out in the fresh air, creating an opening within life.

Gras recounted his tales about his voyages out into the forests of Siberia. He had gone and traversed the Russian Far East by foot, from the north to the south. He orchestrated it in such a way that his descent followed the progression of autumn into the lower latitudes.[2] Escorting the arrival of winter in the forests, he assured the funerary services for the trees. I had to share with him my theory concerning the seasons: until the start of autumn, the forests were indistinct masses where one would have great difficulty distinguishing one tree from the next. Suddenly, autumn arrives and lights its sparks. A given tree with a shorter life cycle embraces the fire and its color changes earlier. Here and there, among the forest canopy, these separate and unique touches of the autumnal flame become individualized, a tree becomes a distinct being, and its light eventually goes out for winter.

In Barjac, we came across the following plaque on a wall in a cemetery: "Passerby, stop and pray, you have arrived at the tomb of the dead. Today, for me. Tomorrow, for you."

The memory of my dead mother caused confusion in reading these sorts of things. Her thoughts accompanied me from out of a vision: why was the memory of those who were no longer among us born from spectacles as anodyne as a tree branch moving in the wind or the outline of the edge of a hill? Suddenly, specters emerge. For several months I wore a ring with a skull on it that was removed by the doctors after my fall. The inscription on the back of the ring pretty much said the same thing as the plaque in the Barjac cemetery: "I was what you were, you will be what I am." I was a bit late in understanding why the Romans had written this inscription at the entrances to their cemeteries. Actually, I was two thousand years late. It was foolish to think that things last forever. Spring mornings were a flash in the pan. It had been quite some time now that I hadn't found myself exactly in the way I had desired: in the midst of movement. I took great joy from standing out in the countryside and slowly advancing on these chosen paths. Invisible, luminous, and clear. Such was the noble lesson drawn by Karen Blixen on her farm in Africa: "I feel good here, right where I should be." Such was the crucial question in life—as simple as it was often neglected.

We tried to circumvent "things," as old folks would say, stratified buttes piercing the plateaus. The landscape mixed the intelligence of village installations with the pleasantness of the reliefs. At Véyrac, we were already dying of thirst. The village was completely empty since the villagers were out milking their cows and we couldn't find any fountain to drink from. At Chasserans, the fountain appeared to be completely dried up and so we asked an old farmer.

"Does this fountain no longer grant water, sir?"

"The peasant farmers are kings now. They do what they please. They cut off the water source from my childhood! They redirected it for the cows."

He pointed an accusing finger at a group of tractors in a nearby barn. The machines gave the barn the appearance of a temple to the Glorious Thirty. Our dear old guide didn't seem to realize that the winds had changed, even for property owners.

"Those two living there have a prime spot. They basically own the whole village."

"But you, sir, how do you get by?"

"We live off a herd of about fifty to one hundred sheep, a vegetable garden, and a bit of hunting. My mother sold them everything."

He invited us to the edge of his property and poured us out two liters of water and bid us farewell. In one brief pause in our wandering, we had received an entire summary of the recent chapters of the government report on hyperrurality.

There was the old archivist guarding the entrance to the cave of memories. Farther along one could make out the buildings constructed during the time of Pompidou's prosperity over whose beams recently ruined working-class peasants could toss a piece of rope to tie around their necks. Upon leaving the village, we saw an abandoned farm whose only promise for a future would be for an Englishman to buy up the property and make a fortune growing quinoa.

We regained a berm on the north edge of the Plateau des Hermets. Below a farm could be seen spread out all the way toward the ledge of a recess. In the valley, the lights from Marvejols blanketed the evening. The moon lit up Gévaudan[3] to the north, softly making its way across and above the valley. We made a fire from collected bramble and thought of the girls that were snatched up by the creatures of the night hiding behind the snowdrifts in the eighteenth century. Then we set to snoring close to the burning embers as we promised ourselves new voyages. The next day, Gras would be heading back to Russia before then embarking on a Belorussian boat headed for a mission to Antarctica. Returning to his own invisible paths.

September 22, the Aubrac

I had the heart of the Massif Central in my sights—the land of village secrets and strange writers, mysterious forests, igneous rocks, and beasts of the devil. Here, one could erase one's traces. I would have to make my way climbing toward the north while keeping a distance from the western rim of the Margeride, thus avoiding the sprawling wound of the A75 highway, more commonly referred to as "la Méridienne." I continued with an ever-increasing confidence, for if there was one region in France where I could seek out possible invisible paths, it was certainly there.

My hope was immediately compensated upon leaving the village of Marvejols. To the west of the village rose the Plateau de La Cham, checkered with granite walls and protected by a series of rustic stone structures. The networks of these structures enclosed tiny plots of land. And just as quickly as I had stumbled upon them, the rain began to pour down and I was lost among a labyrinth whose Minotaurs were nothing more than a bunch of cows with long eyelashes.

And then I came to a number of other wooded areas where land consolidation had clearly laid waste to any remnants of ancient village grid patterns. In the commune of Antrenas, one farm owner explained to me that the construction of the A75 in 1975 had completely obliterated any vestiges of communal life. The infrastructural base of La Cham existed at a distance from the major artery created by the highway. The boss there opened the doors to his barn and let me in as the storm jangled on its rooftops. By the light shining through at the front of the barn, I shared my hunks of bread with four scrawny cats who thanked me for the gesture by guaranteeing me a night's sleep without the disturbance of mice.

Each morning the sun would climb over a barrier of cloud cover and struggle to cross the harrow. At noon, there was a sudden explosion of illumination. The Aubrac, caressed by these rays of light, suddenly projected my memory back to the Mongolian steppes. It was a dreamt earth for drunken wandering. On the plateau, I traced a straight line, climbing over the fences (the Parisian in me should be ashamed of such improper escapades!), and passed through the herds. Sometimes, I'd stumble across a giant boulder in the middle of a field or at the summit of a hillock. I saw within this dispersed landscape the abandoned dice of a now forgotten megalithic game once played by giants. Alas, it was nothing more than a flourishing of granite. Even the velour coats of the cows graciously captured the rays of light. In the Aubrac, one would gather one's animals together under an appellation that I had thought was only reserved for people from the Central Asian plain and to which I regrettably didn't belong: "species of vast expanses." I greeted the "flowers of Aubrac" with a wild flick of the hand. The sky unfurled an air of purified gases, cleansed by the rains of the previous evening, the first autumnal drenching. The tall grasses whipped up, electrified by the wind, the sun turned, and the gusts, charged with photons, peeled my dark thoughts clean away, sweeping up and carrying off the shadows in the strong wind currents. I crossed over swamps, climbed up pitches,[4] and arrived at a village of heathers after hours in the drunken topography of the landscape. An old man with a worrisome eye clung tightly to his cane, dazed, with a foot resting on a granite cross. He appeared just as disfigured as I by some sort of facial paralysis. And he appeared to recognize a sort of proximity in my disgrace as he immediately addressed me like an acquaintance or his equal.

"I once lived in Paris," he said. "I was a coalman and barkeep for someone from Auvergne who had a bistro on rue Diderot."

"Ah yes, I recall those coal cellars," I replied.

The man pounded his cane twice on the ground with each phrase, uttering, like Paul Léautaud during his interviews, "Tack! Tack!"

"Then I worked at Les Halles. I moved here for retirement. My sons raise cattle."

"Are they able to make a good living?'

"No, I don't think so. Tack! Tack! But I think they're doing the right thing, because they returned to the village."

Upon leaving the village I saw a notice bearing the inscription: "Danger, rural milieu." Was it a sign to city dwellers that they were entering an area with tough work ahead in the fields?

I made a slight descent following the course of the Truyère River. The reservoir of the 1960s had flooded the valley, and the lake bore a metallic clarity. A suspension bridge linked the sides, and by nightfall I'd end up in Pierrefort to rest for the evening and sleep on the forest bluff at the entrance to the village. It was a strange night during which I dreamt ten times about rolling off the side of the mountain down into the bottom of the valley. Another day in the books, one where I exchanged three sentences with a keeper of the cross, exhausted my energy reserves on a plateau filled with light, and only made contact with asphalt as night fell. Another day credited to a desire to disappear, an antidote against involuntary servitude.

September 25, la Planèze

Something just wasn't right today. My poor mood was the result, in part, of reading the daily newspaper *La Montagne*—a rag in which the writer Alexandre Vialatte no longer published articles—sitting at a table at the bistro of Villefort in front of two cups of coffee that helped to repair the insomnia I had endured the previous evening. "The digital age is an opportunity to reinforce innovation," the article maintained. The article started off on the wrong foot. Nobody understands these sorts of claims. But all the elected officials of the region applauded. They gathered in an assembly at Murol and prepared for the addition of internet access to their region. They were setting the apparatus in place.

"High-speed internet to the rescue in rural areas." Oh, thank heavens! I thought—saved by the very thing that was leading to the shuttering of all the boutiques. "Those who move here ask for internet access before asking about the schools," the mayor of the village explained in an interview for the article. He also took the opportunity to congratulate himself on the opening of what would soon be the first "digitally capable junior high school." The institution of learning would be called Mermoz. No one seemed to mention that the eponymous demigod of the Aeropostale— who spent forty-eight hours in the Andes repairing his plane with nothing but a monkey wrench—would not have much to say about *high-speed internet.* No one seemed to add that placing a *screen* between oneself and the world never seemed to fix anything.

Too much coffee, too much newspaper reading, too many promises of a better world. Too much of this acrid foam that mornings seem to birth in the early hours of a bistro. I had to set off again to let this bitterness dissolve in the sweeping strides of my footsteps. To say that high-speed internet is a rather acceptable solution is fine as long as one equated it to the early creation of tunnels through the caves of Burgundy using hatchets.

All day long, as I walked beneath the low-lying sky, I fulminated against the instability of the paths to be taken, where only the vultures tracking the voles from high above seemed to be enjoying themselves. Configuring knowledgeable routes on a map to help myself overcome the obstacles of a dying and abandoned dead-end croplands made me foam at the mouth. My IGN (Institut Geographique National) maps still contained the ancient cadastral traces of the paths once used by former peasants. The property owners no longer had to hide the ease with which they were quick to manage old paths and swallow them whole within the confines of their plots of land. On the slopes that led to the Col de Prat de Bouc, I shared my map with a farmer who was tinkering with his fence.

"I don't think it's a private-access road," I said, showing him the sketched path I was looking for.

"You won't find those paths any longer. You're looking at old maps," he replied.

"No," I said. "These are the most current edition of the maps from this year."

"Well, then, those are really old routes you are seeking out and we must have modified them."

I stopped around noon in the shadows of the calvaries. I began working on the flexibility exercises that my physical therapists referred to as "the Mohammedan position," consisting of stretching one's back muscles in a kneeling position on the ground. The density of the number of crosses around these plateaus was remarkable. In the city, the admirers of Robespierre called for a radical extension of secularity. Some among them were militant and advocated the outright removal of nativity scenes from public spaces during the Christmas holiday season. These fierce spirits fascinated me. Were they even aware that the Christian cross was scattered a hundred times over across the summits of France? Or that calvaries were nailed at thousands of crossroads in the countryside? In the forest, in the hollows of certain tree trunks, even at the backs of caves, tiny statuettes of saints resided next to nocturnal spiders. Oftentimes mountain climbers would even tie their ropes to lead statues of the Virgin Mary that were soldered into the granite to make their rappels from the mountain crags. As luck would have it, the adorers of Reason were too busy reading Ravachol to have time to climb up the mountainsides with their leisurely, doe-like footsteps. If I held a fondness for this tinware of faith, it's not so much because I believed in the morose fable of a unique God, nor that I feared or lamented the sway of parish priests. Rather, I didn't appreciate the fact that people always seemed to lash out at what is already standing upright. Furthermore, among all the symbols that man has invented to illustrate his tales, I just didn't think the cross and statues of the Virgin Mary populating these high altitudes were the worst among them. We shouldn't simply uproot things if we don't have something better to replace them with. Any French park ranger could eruditely explain this to any agnostic.

4

THE INVISIBLE
SHADOWS

September 28, Monts du Cantal

At Murat, once again I no longer found myself alone. My friend
Humann showed up to join me for a stretch. After the departure
of Gras, another wind from Russia blew near me again. Of all my
friends, Arnaud Humann was the only one of them who really
knew how to cut his ties with the rest of the world. He had lived
now for more than thirty years in Siberia without any other secure
abode that served as some sort of back-up dwelling. He lived his
life by only one principle: traveling without any baggage whatsoever. Not a single ruble to his name, but he had accumulated a
treasure chest full of memories. Every time he returned to France,
he was always dumbfounded to see how great numbers of his own
countrymen had convinced themselves they were a shining light
for the rest of the world. His friends of the Taiga were perhaps a
bit brutish, but their lone ambitions were to stay warm throughout the winter. This seemed to garner a people less terrified by
notions of universalism but also replete with a conviviality that
led to the most splendid and welcoming of evening gatherings. A
protective layer in the event of drunken jeremiads. For more than
twenty years, Humann had traversed and cut his way through
the landscape and coastlines of Kamchatka, the delta of Love,

the taigas of Yakutia, and the ice fields of Baikal. On the edge of the Lena River he married Taniouchka and admitted that he had somehow crossed over into another way of life. And with that, he carried himself with fierce blue eyes and the gait of a bear.

He would accompany me for the next several days on foot. He was brimming with excitement to be cutting his way through the French landscape instead of the immensity of the Siberian terrain, which typically left one overwhelmed and with no hope of any variation in the landscape. We left Murat, a village of dark stones, and headed upward 15 kilometers to the summit of the Plomb du Cantal. At that altitude, the sea of clouds was a true delight for Humann. He embraced everything that camouflaged the world: clouds, distance, and vodka. We would redescend toward the ski resort at Super Lioran. The installations there left their marks and gashes on the slopes. They did not uproot or disorient Humann, accustomed as he was to the singular brilliance of old Soviet implementations of land management and the cultivation of green spaces.

Why was it already two o'clock in the afternoon? And why were we where we were instead of somewhere else? As we sat peacefully on the grass in the shadows of the concrete buildings at the ski resort, quietly eating a lunch of a hunk of bread, a desire to die arose from deep inside me. It overcame me slowly, like an evil spell suddenly emerging on the horizon. A dark stain invaded my being like cuttlefish ink darkening the waters of the sea. Later, having regained my senses, I recalled a friend from Val-d-Isère who had regaled me with tales of traversing the Atlantic Ocean in a sailboat. Somewhere out in the middle of her voyage, she plunged into the ocean and could see an (inoffensive) whale shark rising up from out of the deep beneath her. For a moment, she was completely paralyzed, deprived of all her reflexes. The shadow I could sense being born and rising up from out of my own depths, felt something like a beast, but not like a beautiful sea creature:

more like a horrific monster. What I had experienced was, in fact, an episode of epilepsy: a dark evil.

The fractures of my skull would at times provoke epileptic seizures. In the firetruck that eventually took me to Aurillac, I began to return to normal and saw Humann's friendly face staring back at me while the vehicle swerved down the road.

"You started convulsing in the grass," he said.

"It never lasts that long," I replied.

"It was still thirty minutes . . . and it wasn't pleasant to see."

"No, it wasn't a pleasant experience," I agreed. "I would wager that it happened because we're now in a landscape with lava underfoot. There is fire underneath this basalt. This ground is pulsating with evil vibrations. Epilepsy is fatal on volcanic soil."

"That is another valid explanation," Humann concurred.

September 29

I spent the night at the hospital in Aurillac and was given the OK to leave by the neurologists the following morning at ten. An immediate urgency overcame me to once again set about walking, to conjure the shadows and eventually attain the sea in order to cast off the cliffs the poisons that had led to my fall the previous year. I attempted to summon the invisible paths to bequeath me one last distillation of their ambrosia. What I had asked of them only continued to increase. I had beseeched them to provide an opening into rural France, to educate me in the art of dissimulation, to get me back up and moving again. At present, I needed to clear the paths clean of this epileptic ink. So it was that I confirmed the magical character of this walk, whose conclusion alone would engender my complete and total recovery. Holding to one's promises was the best of remedies.

The doctors had not formally forbidden me to set off on long walks out in the landscape again, but they had also not ardently suggested I do so. We tend to forget that doctors are often unher-alded diplomats. Personally, I couldn't help but think of the words of Vialatte: "An escargot never recoils." Occasionally phrases such as this are the best prescriptions during difficult times.

A taxi drove us back to the exact place where I had lost con-sciousness. Under the noonday sun, we set off again on the great hiking path of Pas de Peyrol and continued walking seven hours until night fell on a plateau marked by herds of sheep and isolated shepherds' huts. The air was frenzied, mad, and arrogant. The wind distributed its slaps throughout the tall grasses, disturbing the blond manes of horses, and rendered the sky furious. The Monts du Cantal delineated the landscape into one long undula-tion. One thing was certain: those mountains were stable. Having exited once more from neurological obscurity, I felt alive again because I was back out on the road. A feeling of a perfected purity. We took a break and set up camp in the woods where sunlight still penetrated through the penumbra. Humann was a perfect friend, and he fashioned the perfect campsite for someone still trying to recover from having their head rattled: a pre-Raphaelian light, soft, mossy ground, dinner around some tree stumps, and the friendship of owls that were already beginning to hoot in the early evening. We fell asleep under the gleam of their eyes.

September 30, crossing the Artense plateau

A mild and dry night under the ancient tree canopy worked its magic. A miracle. I awoke at the foot of a pine tree, brimming with a rekindled enthusiasm. Does a tree somehow bestow a bit of its vital force on the organism of the individual who sleeps at its foot? After all, we often gain something positive and vital by remaining in close proximity with certain beings. Perhaps the same could be said about one's relationship with trees.

We spent hours finding ways to crawl through fences, some-times opening and closing them in order to clear a path through the fields. The water voles scurried toward their subterranean lodging. The birds of prey kept them in their sights from above. The conifers maintained their freshness. And the paths spread throughout the forest between stone hedges. Autumn had achieved its victory over the ferns: they were already weeping. They were the first reminders that the party was over. The trees, however, remained. And the granite was flush with moss. Such wondrous landscapes were not lost on the local tourism office, which then decided to bestow upon the region the name "little Scandinavia." However, as we traversed a myriad of tiny villages, silence reigned, and we didn't encounter one single Swedish maiden in mini shorts.

At Condat, one could not be faulted for mistaking that a national day of mourning had been declared. What in fact had happened in just over five decades to these localities of place-names?

"It's as if the Russians were arriving," joked Humann.

Journeying through these villages gave one the impression of half-heartedly paging through a real estate brochure. What wasn't already closed was for sale. What was for sale couldn't find any buyers. The monuments to the dead bore gloriously poetic names, and it seemed that the small number of people strolling through the cobbled streets could certainly have their names added to the list. The only businesses that appeared to still be flourishing were beauty salons. The signs in the window seemed to be saying, "When the ship has been all but abandoned, at least we can still make one more last beauty for the road!" Narcissism still nourished the economy. And there we were, smack dab in the middle of nowhere, in the gray zones of "hyperrurality." The inhabitants of this desert had convinced themselves that Paris was not listening to them. One got the sense that an entire people had very recently embarked on an exodus, emptying out the area. In Australia, the spider wasp, a sumptuous creature with a rubicund outer shell, lays its eggs inside a living tarantula. The wasp's larvae will then eventually devour the spider from the inside as they grow. Ah, the trifold apparatus of the glorious economy, industrial agriculture, and a triumphant urbanism was its very own wasp spider of the countryside.

A horrible idea suddenly began to grip me: what if my bout of epilepsy was caused by a relapse of melancholy? I immediately told Humann that we needed to quickly find our way back onto a path surrounded by trees, throwing ourselves back into the forest timber, rejoining the currents and flows of the water sources, and extracting ourselves from these pallid dead zones.

Was I swerving a bit into nostalgia? Humann certainly seemed convinced of it.

"You're spoiled," he muttered.

"So what?" I replied.

Was it so wrong to think a village with an orchestra of oom-pahs and the low rumbling of mooing cattle possessed a bit more poetry within its streets than a boulevard replete with blinking neon signs advertising manicures? Up until now, I had been the enemy of such backward-looking, old-fashioned thinking. Fearing the contagion of cheesiness, I had considered nostalgia a shame-ful malady, far worse than cirrhosis of the liver, which still seemed like a fair trade and price to pay for an unknown quantity of joyous evenings. I forced myself to believe that the "France of the hills," according to the geographer Pierre George, was nothing more than a memory—or worse—a dream. Each innovation owed it-self the task of rendering happiness. Moreover, my argument was foolproof: in Horace, Rousseau, Nerval, and Lévi-Strauss one un-covers the same regret for the flow of time, proof that nostalgia was nothing more than the stammerings of the senile, the lament-ing of no longer being twenty years old. Talent, on the other hand, consisted in becoming passionate about the soubresauts of the current age. Take Cocteau, for instance! He had sparked new flames of culture, applauded the artistic eruptions and inno-vations of the era. But the past few months had changed me, and this brief walk within the decor of the countryside had only accel-erated my reform. From now on, I would no longer be ashamed of admitting my nostalgia for that which I hadn't experienced or known. I had developed an appreciation for the smell of tannin, reddened mountain faces, and long wooden tables sitting beneath the wooden beams of a barn. I loved the substance of things, the music of objects, the promise of evenings adorned with paper lanterns. And this particular song of the world was not to be heard in the surrounding corridors. Was it not a bit inappropriate to attempt to establish a hierarchy among things? To prefer the France of Roupnel—albeit a pure fantasy—to the rows upon rows of abandoned and perished village dwellings?

In passing through the Dordogne, we knocked on a farm door requesting a bit of water. On the wooden table in their humble abode, they set us down two cups of coffee and Humann began to regale our gracious host about the Russian forests and how they became fatigued by the onset of winter. As for our host, a farmer, he told us a story I had heard before on several occasions: a childhood spent in the countryside, an adult life in the city, and the subsequent return to a landscape that had been all but erased. The front door began to creak open.

"Ah, my son," our host explained.

A man in blue silently acknowledged our presence and greeted his father. The bare lightbulb hanging from the ceiling flashed swirling in front our faces.

"You see, I was first a son and then the father of a farmer," the old man exclaimed.

Between the two, a parenthesis, a life. "When I was a kid, we always kept four or five cows. We made three rounds of Saint-Nectaire cheese per day. Today, they make 150 per day."

I did not know exactly what sort of technological machinery was required for such phenomena, nor did I possess the requisite intellectual ability to analyze them. But I could sense that our host was getting right to the important elements of the matter at hand. A feeling of no longer inhabiting one's earthly dwelling with the same grace as before arising out of a profound and overall trepidation based on growth. Suddenly, there was too much of everything. Too much production, too much movement, too many forms of energy.

Such effects inside a brain provoked epilepsy. In History, such happenings are called mass industrialization. In society, such processes lead to a crisis.

October 3, near the community of Ussel

Humann left me at Ussel and headed back to his Russian loves. His last words to me waiting on the train platform: "I can't miss the 2:50 train from Ussel to Irkutsk." I kept my line heading northward by way of woods and pasturelands. In the forest, the path was unrelenting. The herons flew high above, crackling through the branches at the forest's edge. I walked for six straight hours. The rain pursued my path and propelled me onward. It poured down. Hardly any air between the drops. In the village of La Courtine, the police stopped me.

"We're going to have to ask for your papers, please," they said.

"Holy cow! The constabulary has suddenly become rather friendly," I thought to myself as I fumbled through my backpack looking for my ID. The two sentries turned and escorted me to a tiny hotel 200 hundred meters farther down the road. I was a bit annoyed for having distracted these officials of public service by my own leisure activities. And for the second time, after a journey in a firetruck, I found myself sitting in the back of an official vehicle. The owner of the hotel looked me over with a bit of suspicion. There isn't a single innkeeper or hotel manager who appreciates a potential client getting out of a paddy wagon.

The gunfire I heard the following day while walking through the forest explained the zeal of the police officers. The military camp at La Courtine made use of its enchanted valleys, and they were therefore off-limits to foreigners like me who are not part of the military. One could picture the myriad salamanders, barn owls, and other creatures attempting to hide themselves every time another round of 120 mm mortar fire was unleashed.

I often slept in the fields. The rain would not immediately awaken me. I'd prop one eye open once the water droplets began to drench my clothing a bit and I could feel the icy cold creep up across my shoulder blade. I considered this a form of proof of the high quality of sleep one can attain lying on plowed land. Through the department of the Creuse, I wandered in a state of dry inebriation. The medicine circulating in my veins to combat epilepsy left me in a bit of a daze, along with the doses of colchicine for cardiac complications and other products to calm the pain in my legs. I had set my life on fire, burned all my dwellings and bridges, jumped out of the way to avoid getting burned, and at the present moment, I wandered down the invisible paths with a general inflammation that the medicine was able to keep contained. "Try not to fall into the water," I reminded myself as I walked across the bridges over creeks. "It would probably be a good idea to avoid chemically polluting the water table of the region."

October 5, on the Millevache plateau

These were melancholy days, less whipped up with swirling photons than those previous days in Provence. Less swept up in the ardor of traversing the mountain passes. They were filled with crowning the rounded hilltops of a more timid landscape, castles with closed shutters resembling the decor of *Le Grand Meaulnes* for cousins blushing in their cotton chinos.[1] I found the paths between the hills rather peaceful. The horses in the fields came galloping over as I passed through the pastureland, a sign that they were not accustomed to seeing that many folks around here. They came to spend a brief friendly moment together during solitary hours. The valleys were hot and humid: the sexual organs of the topographical relief. The toads looked on from their retreats. The wind rose, brushing up against the forest. I hovered between splendid views of the countryside worthy of illustrations by Vidal de La Blache and deserted villages. When I found myself on empty roads, I posed the same question as that of the ship-wrecked upon waking up in the midst of the sea surrounded by rubble, resting on one last piece of wood: where did everybody go? I traversed Magnat-l'Étrange (Magnate-the-Strange), whose name served to magnetize me, even though it could have been called *Magnat-le-délaissé* (Magnate-the-abandoned).

Sometimes, on these bald hilltops, a bakery resisted and persisted. The boutique would take on several other responsibilities, such as carrying items one would normally find in a regular grocery store, even becoming the site for the post office, as well as the tobacco shop. Certain bakeries were no better stocked than a Moldovan merchant during the Soviet era: a can of tuna, a jar of artichoke hearts, Tagada Strawberries, and some AA batteries. At 10 o'clock in the morning at Cugnat, the merchant was on the telephone: "No, I don't have any more bread, all that's left is one tarte." These were discussions about rations!

One could uncover such places as this among the trading posts of the Polynesian atolls where sea vagabonds, having disembarked from their vessels, came to toss back a couple of shots of rum and inquire into the current state of affairs of the world. They would take advantage of their respite on land to purchase jugs of motor oil and several meters of rope. Here, in the French countryside of the Limousin, the irony was found in the fact that these last surviving trading posts were funded by the European Union. The flag of the EU whipped in the wind on every city hall with its closed shutters. The butchers of the old French expanse took to occupying themselves with sewing back together the cadaver of the countryside to whose demise they had themselves contributed.

October 7, near the Haute Marche

Sometimes I would leave the forests for three or four kilometers to walk on the road, between two tangles in the invisible paths. Some of the passing drivers would make a hand gesture as if to dust off the road, or worse: they honked their horns. It was a rather unfair situation since the internal combustion engine had only quite recently established its supremacy over the practice of walking. As such, the pedestrian should have taken a bit of joy from its historical precedence.

In the barns, one could note the bales of hay had already been arranged for winter. Aligned into robust golden circles, they provoked reveries of bountiful gatherings with dumplings. At Mourzines, I furtively slept on the steps of the church before seeking out a bistro where I could toss back a couple of shots of Viandox since my days of hammering shots of schnapps to get the creative juices flowing were now over.

Farewell, pints of draft beer! So long, my dear friend wine! My life now belonged to water! In the bars upon pushing the door open, the regulars, while never hostile, would immediately size me up, and often betray a slight demeanor of astonishment. Was it my deformed facial features? My accoutrements? I was the guy who ordered a cup of soup while lugging around a backpack, with his mouth oddly askew, gripping his trekking poles, basically the spitting image of a tourist. And once I announced that I was "from Paris" to the gentleman sitting in front of his beer who posed the question, I could already sense the old country sarcasm for the city-slicker whom he often held in contempt. In such instances, I would think back to my time spent in Tuscany with the baroness of an olive orchard, Beatrice von Rezzori, in the north of Florence. Once, I took Beatrice by car to the village olive press when it was time to start the machine and watch several tons of Santa Maddalena olives make their way across into the machine to be pressed. Beatrice, carefully paying attention to each step in the process, was rather at ease among the peasants. Eleven o'clock later that evening, she would have to be seated at the ambassadors' table. What I witnessed, among the sweet and delicate odors of auriferous liquid, was a certain familial conviviality between the princes of life and the workers of the earth. In that moment, a decorative fraternity had yet to be fractured by class struggle. Basically, I beheld a romantic dream.

October 9, in the department of La Creuse

As the sky began to open up, I was setting off with majestic strides. I had acquired a habit, instituted a new ritual that I recommend to any walker among the thickets. In hurtling myself toward the meadow at the edge of the forest, I would shout out at the top of my lungs: "Who among you watches the borders?" And sometimes I would see a frightened deer, a pheasant, a jackrabbit, or a wading bird swooping down—proof that my call was not in vain and that the kingdom's periphery was still under a certain protection by a valiant group of sentinels. Borders are the very ramparts between empires.

I traversed the charming hamlet of Hérat, populated by the Dutch, who appeared to spend their time growing balconies. I had taken Hérat to be the name of a city in western Afghanistan where self-immolations by women frequently took place. I thought to myself that toponymy is a rather peculiar science where the same name is handed out to designate both charming locales and cursed cities. Perhaps better reasoning could be afforded here: perhaps not all partook in the same grace when they set about creating the conditions for happiness according to the rules they established for themselves.

A man in a straw hat waved to me from his garden. He was from Amsterdam. "We've settled down here, because there's pretty much nobody left. There's one old woman who has been abandoned here for whom we cook dinner." What a lesson! These

Protestants from the north found the means to apply the virtues of social democracy in the confines of their retirement. Their program could bear the title humanitarians and secondary residence.

The forests were increasingly mutating into their golden hues, and the rowan tree punctuated the changing of the seasons with a dash of red. The apple trees crumbled under the remaining fruit, their contours lending hints of a Japanese russet to the periphery. The wind wrenched the last remaining gleaming speckles from the trees surrounding the moats. The remnants of the trees turned into piles of wood chips upon hitting the ground, like motifs from a Klimt painting. I would have exchanged one of my big toes to have a discussion with a professor from the Louvre walking alongside me so as to provide, with each glimpse of my gaze, a course on the history of landscape painting. Why was it that it took so long for European painters to take leave from their studios and plant their easels out in the open landscape? Why did they wait so long to invite the rest of the world into their artworks? It is rather probable that receiving beautiful young women to pose nude in one's atelier leads to not having much desire to leave one's abode.

For a long time, religious motifs were the only ones to be authorized by those in power. Medieval man belonged to God, painting expressed the sacred. Then the Renaissance liberated inspiration. The Flemish began to paint their countryside. Pieter Bruegel the Elder took ice-skaters and tiny ducks as the subjects of his paintings. And before him, certain artists had figured out a way to subvert the demands of the Church by inventing veduta. They would carefully orchestrate a view of some sacred scene near a window where they could then deploy a wilder perspective of everyday, ordinary life. The Virgin and the Child would be seated next to a window from which one could glimpse flowing serpentine rivers. A master of the Italian Renaissance, Bernardino Luini, had represented the Virgin Mary alongside Saint Elizabeth, the former holding an enormous baby Jesus on her knee and the latter, a chubby Saint John the Baptist. The entire lot of them were placed in the middle of a luxurious forest so lifelike one could almost hear the rustling of the branches in the wind. I imagined that Christ would have certainly loved to make off with his friends to go play in the forest. A new motivation for escaping out onto the invisible paths: escaping conventions, passing through the veduta, and making one's way into the forests hiding in the background.

The break I had been waiting for finally came several kilometers north of the village of Vigoulant. One final slope led to a fold in the terrain and then gave way to the birth of the plains. The horizon offered up its promises; the sky benevolently covered the entirety of the earth. I made my way from the region of Limousin to Centre, from the department of Creuse to the department of Indre. I was finally done traversing the granite-laden terrain surrounded by carefully tailored shadowy ravines where future presidents of the Republic were incubating. I extracted myself from the Massif Central. Oh, I had yet to arrive in the lands of royal France, the lands of feudal plains and game hunting alongside the Loire River. But I had already arrived at the flat and blessed town of Berry. The farmers here would be less worrisome, the earth less rough, the brambles less vigorous, and the snakes less sure of their rights. From here, I'd begin sketching out my path toward the northwest with my sights set on Cotentin, thereby leaving the strictly "hyperrural" geography deemed as such by the government report. If I had really wanted to comply with the rules I had set for myself, I would have simply set off for the Ardennes by way of Allier, Nièvre, and Yonne. Seeking out invisible paths in a more modernized and Jacobin region made the game a bit more complicated. I'd be better off carefully examining each site and uncovering the hidden paths.

The open space of the landscape in front of me spurred me onward with a newfound vigor; the relief somehow dictated my mood by virtue of some sort of geopsychic phenomena.

October 10, the region of Boischaut-Sud

As for the plains, the hay had disappeared, and the fields were no longer mere enclosed spaces. The labyrinth opened up onto the heart of France. The villages were grouped together, and I followed long forests paths or stayed close to the edges of the fields. Songs began to arise from deep inside me and make their way up to my lips. They had lingered for months down in my throat, seeking a safe passage up into my mouth.

Peasant work in the open field requires an enormous amount of collective effort. In such tiny local communities, a family laboring together could perhaps be sufficient. A former sociologist and a master of backward theories had once proclaimed that agricultural systems could in fact determine one's political affiliations. He claimed that residing in a tiny locality enlarged one's mind. Peasants surrounded by bales of hay all day long were more disposed to welcoming a stranger so as to break with their daily solitude. The villagers of the open fields had everything to lose from an influx of strangers. They dreamt of ramparts since they hardly had anything of the sort. Those towns that were structured within a citadel could allow themselves to set a place at the table for a poor traveler and await his arrival. In other words, one suffered more from globalization out on the plains than within the walls of a fortified village.

The tractor drivers began to sow their crops. They must have incredible inner lives in order to spend hour upon hour making trips back and forth, up and down their same plots of land. Only Schubert—or was it Beethoven?—thought that farm laborers were content and happy in their daily toil. They perhaps possessed a certain depth, but combing hundreds of kilometers plowing the furrows of the land, at full speed, couldn't possibly make you a merry soul. But they kept at it, with a cloud of birds in tow, following closely behind them, come to dine on the earthworms laid bare by the machine.

"They look like seabirds following in the wake of a fishing boat," Daphné exclaimed.

My sister had met up with me the day before at La Châtre. I had promised her a ride on a calm train. The evenings will be serene, I had said. We will take short days on our walk, and it will make for a comfortable evening sleeping under the stars. She could return to Paris the following day.

"I've never slept outside before," she reminded me when we met each other at the train station.

"We'll find a nice clearing, make a good fire, and prepare dinner. You'll feel more at home than at the Palazzo Ducale."

As night fell, right before we made our way up the butte of the Lys castle, we asked an old woman if we were heading in the proper direction, and the conversation veered toward the old village washhouse.

"I used to beat the laundry clean with all the other women in town at the washhouse. Now's there's washing machines. I still pass by the old place where we used to gather and watch my memories flow."

Before the evening had finally set in, I found the forest around the castle. Trees always tend to offer a safe refuge, the ground was flat, and we set about putting Daphné's tent together. The bread was grilling nicely on the fire, the air was peaceful, everything seemed to be going well. And that's when they attacked. I had spent thousands of nights camping under the stars on various latitudes, and the one night that I spend with my younger sister suddenly began to resemble a visit from a ghost train.

I had accidentally made the fire directly beneath a hornets' nest. They began buzzing around in the darkness, got caught in our hair, circled a couple of times around our fire, and then plunged into the flames like Japanese Zero planes crashing into warships in the Pacific. All we needed to do was simply stay still, but Daphné decided it was a better idea to run screaming back to her tent. She sought refuge in her sleeping bag, where a spider was awaiting her. Several hornets made their way into the tent and then things really became uncontrollable. One hour later, I felt it was necessary to tell my sister that the cries echoing throughout the forest were not from some half-mad little girl in a white dress but were merely the calls of a barn owl.

October 11, the Indre River

Hours came and went among the forests of the central zone of France. Following the invisible paths here consisted of connecting back up to the last happy little island remnants of remaining reefs of gallic selva. Under the natural naves, it snowed yellow-leaf tears. The air smelled of a mysterious humidity and moss. I crossed paths with horsemen and deer, hunters who had acquired a specific scientific knowledge (with the notion of obtaining a hunting license) for distinguishing the former from the latter.

Between two trees, I cried out my undying love songs to the cows and sometimes received a long *mooooh* in response.

At Sainte-Sévère, I read the newspapers beneath an oily sun. The news of the global current events was no worse than normal. After all, when Attila set off with the Huns on the banks of the Loire, the situation certainly couldn't have been any more enviable than today.

In the Ardennes, the Indre flowed gently, powerfully, flaked with golden leaves. Autumn was beginning to cover the rivers with leopard motifs. The contemplation of the current sent peaceful memories vibrating to my inner depths. I began to wonder if rivers as well ever felt a certain nostalgia for their source.

Upon leaving the village I stumbled across a bar where I ordered a cup of bouillon.

"Where are you headed?" the barkeep asked.

"To Châteauroux, on foot," I replied.

"That's quite a ways from here. Don't order a Viandox. It will only make you sleepy."

"OK, then, what should I order?"

"A beer."

"Beer is off-limits," I explained. "Doctor's orders."

And then I began to think how nice it would be to toss back a couple of glasses of white wine so as to feel a certain grandeur grow deep down inside me. A friendly void. I would gently lean on the bar and watch in amazement as my thoughts took shape, becoming tiny characters in a carnival. I would take to conversing with my fellow comrades seated there. They would become blood brothers since our blood would have been irrigated with the same chemical composition. The glass of water and the bowl of Viandox deprived me of such fraternal inclinations. One of those drinking at the bar wanted nevertheless to provide me with his council: "Take the bus and drink anyway!"

October 12, in the Champagne de Châteauroux

I stayed the night in a hotel in Châteauroux. A hotel in Châteauroux! This expression recalled to mind something out of vaudeville stage direction, and the simple evocation of this episode from now on will always make me think I have become one of Labiche's bourgeoise.

At daybreak, my dear friend Thomas Goisque would arrive at the train station with his backpack, and on our way out of town we would immediately pass through a succession of completely empty neighborhoods on the edges of the Indre River.

Goisque's father had recently passed away. He was going to walk with me for a couple of days to leave his despair on the side of the road with each passing step, allowing us to reconnect and renew our friendship of the past ten years by partaking in adventures we had embarked on together.

"My old friend, times have changed!" I said.

"How so?"

"Ten years ago, you and I, between Kabul and Kathmandu, to eventually land in Châteauroux: what a disaster!"

A photographer, he had traveled throughout sixty countries as a reporter, particularly in Southeast Asia. We often met up in the Gobi Desert, on the Tibetan plateau, or on Lake Baikal. The Indre River? It was our first time.

The first day we slogged out forty kilometers to set up camp for the evening, not too far from Châteauroux. We had actually tracked back over some of the trail we had already traversed, but our path was beautiful, and one was apt to zigzag a bit if one was going to walk out in the darkness of night.

Under the poplars, we evoked the dead: his father, my mother. We didn't share the same recourse for consolations. He had God and I had to be satisfied with the world. What was the safer choice? To believe in the eternity of some paradise, or to seek out the shadows of the dead within the folds of nature? This topic preoccupied much of our discussions, but the gulf was wide and would not be overcome. As for myself, I took to imagining that the memory of my mother sometimes manifested itself in the reflections of a pond. My dear friend Goisque, however, was certain and relieved in knowing that his father was peacefully inhabiting a nearby locale where he would one day join him. We weren't even going to try to convince each other.

We traversed the rocky plains. The hills and their beveled edges pointed toward the sky, offering up to the light a bounty of beautiful, fertile flatlands. The air smelled of mushrooms. The landscape shared similarities with that of Champagne.

For four straight days, we journeyed along the banks of the Indre. The river unfurled its silk through the hay of the poplars and willows. We took in the river's presence. It shimmered with light, retracted into the shadows, returned, and then vanished again. We sought out good places to camp on the islands in the undergrowth. I almost began to fear disturbing the tutelary fairies. We set up our table on top of stumps in whose bark slept velvet-skinned sala-manders. We erected a shelter to conceal our campfires so as to not add to the farmers' fear of the Roma creating misfortunes for them. Goisque sharpened tree branches into spears to cook the sausages he had brought along, and we began to understand why the Russians loved to grill meat in the forest: a campfire was an escape. We drunkenly gorged ourselves on the food, and there was no ear in sight to hear our conversations. Slabs of cooked meat and freedom. After the luxury of spending nights around a campfire under the stars, sleeping in a palace later on practically becomes unbearable.

During the day, we sought out supplies in tiny sleepy villages. Finding a café that was open was the equivalent of seeking out an oasis south of Ouarzazate. Clion-sur-Indre and Villedieu had been struck down by a dark spell. Fate had bestowed on them an affliction of a national highway. A bloodletting within the fat of the countryside. A thirty-three-ton noria traversing an empty buffer zone.

At Villedieu, under the tympanum of a nineteenth-century church, one could make out in dark letters the following inscription: La République Française.

"All that nonsense from Father Combes!" muttered Goisque.[2]

Upon arriving at Clion-sur-Indre, we found the following lovely banner: "Rural: sub-citizens of the Republic."

"It's an ad campaign against the fusion of projects created by collectivities. You know what's going to collapse within that whole fusion? Business as we know it!" exclaimed Goisque.

The country was just like its antagonists: not happy with the idea of change. Time shuffled its playing cards, History advanced onward, and old structures crumbled. In the countryside as much as in the highest offices of the State, the establishment vacillated. No one could predict what would happen next. No one enjoys the intermission, and no one seemed to like the idea of residing in a Philip K. Dick short story. And yet the forest remained a way to spend an enjoyable evening. The invisible paths remained as well for a way to have a bit of fun.

The railroad from Loches to Châteauroux that had fallen into disuse in the 1970s slithered its way from one bank to the next. We followed its last remnants for several kilometers, dusted off the footbridges surrounded by shrubbery, crossed over metallic bridges that had been tossed out over the Indre during the postwar period. We hobbled over the joists and forced our way through the thickets toward the northernmost point. The brambles inundated the rails—the undergrowth being the first to reconquer the wilderness. After having penetrated through all that, we looked at the undergrowth with a different eye. I started to have a profound admiration for the prickly plants.

"I prefer civilizations with cultivated fields. What can I say?" Goisque chimed.

The moment was a bit quixotic: a path was disappearing and we felt great because it offered us no hope whatsoever. Merely a propulsion bestowed by dreams.

Beaulieu-lès-Loches, Azay-sur-Indre: the river unfurled its caresses. At daybreak, we were awakened by the crows (anonymously, of course), and we set back off into the landscape. The landscape left one with the impression of a subtle gentleness, beholding a great ancient secret, of some distant indolence. It was a land for timid birds. Even the various waterways gently brushed up against their banks with a loving grace. Driven mad by the odors emanating from the baked goods we had purchased at the boulangerie, only the shrews seemed to be endowed with a certain boldness when they'd stomp across our backpacks left on the ground at the campsite. Our conversations eventually brought us to our shared obsession: the invisible paths. Goisque knew very well that these paths often led us out into areas not located on the cartographies of the geographers and that these drift passages would slowly but surely drill their galleries and tunnels into us, deep down inside. It was difficult to make oneself into a monastery, but once one had lifted up the hatch of one's interior crypt, the journey was certainly viable. I had procured a great passion for all human forms of experience of withdrawal. Individuals who threw themselves into the world with the intention of changing it certainly fascinated me, but something always kept me at a distance from such endeavors: they always ended up manifesting a satisfaction with themselves. They made speeches, constructed theories, drew crowds of people: they chose the paths of light. Prepared to consider life as some sort of staircase and in sharp contrast to the dancers in revues who descended the stairwell by explosions from their pens in hopes of garnering applause, I preferred the lighthouse keepers whose slow and labored steps scraped the ground as they climbed back up the stairs to their towers.

There have been one and a million ways to flee the world. A man from the Paleolithic era must have been the first to launch the movement. I began to imagine him getting up off the ground, leaving behind the halo of fire, forever disappearing out into the savanna, forever under threat but free. Later down the road, History began to multiply such experimentations. Port-Royal was the noblest and most accomplished way of taking leave from the world. The Cistercian monastery was the most relaxed form: everything was already set in place, meals were served at regular hours. The most modest form was to have a study: all one needed was a love of erudition and a desk. The atelier of the artist was perhaps the most civilized form: one withdrew from the world and left an oeuvre to posterity. The most hedonistic form was perhaps seeking refuge in the mountains: in case of boredom, one set off up the north face simply for the beauty of the gesture. The most painful: the hermit's cave—eating lizards during the fourth century. The most romantic form was clearly that taken by shepherds in the alpine meadows. The cabin in the woods being, of course, the most juvenile. The form of withdrawal with the most class had to be the colonial fort, the outposts of empire. The riskiest had to be the commune, having another go at the farming body, since the State certainly did not care for such islands of potential contestation. The writer Élisabeth Barillé recently presented a novel method of withdrawal: she affirmed that her partial deafness "condemned her to an adventure of depths."[3] All that remained was for those beings appalled by the ugliness of the world to simply gouge out their eyes.

All these recluses had made use of their invisible paths to gain ground toward some inner regions of solitude. They refused the accumulation of objects, were opposed to the projection of the world onto a screen. The anarchists from Tarnac, the starets from medieval Russia, and the méharistes of the former French West Africa would perhaps not have accepted conversing with each other. And yet, they all resembled each other: populating a desert was not something uncongenial with their demeanors, they all were fairly thin, and each one understood rather well that the enemy often appeared suddenly from out of the void.

Goisque left my side a bit south of Tours, on the edges of the Indre, and I continued my way heading northward under a lukewarm sky. The air smelled of recently extinguished altar candles and the coats of gray cats: the scent of autumn. A pastel light hovered over the fields. I was moving along with a bit more flexibility than had been the case at the beginning of my voyage. Walking had begun to distill its positive effects. It had bequeathed to me this treasure that I had been in such great need of and which I had so little knowledge of how to conserve: rhythm. Sometimes I would breathe in the air above the fields in wondrous gulps. Could one become intoxicated by the scent of fields washed at night like one could from a good bottle of dry red wine? There was something stimulating about the inhalations from these freshly cut fields: a sign that the earth was breathing and that I still possessed the ability to tread upon it. While staying at a bed-and-breakfast in Azay-sur-Indre, I discovered a book about the history of the penal colony in Cayenne, French Guiana. I also came across the antiphony of those condemned there: "The past betrayed me, the present torments me, the future horrifies me." Walking in the woods swept away these fears. I perhaps could also compose a ritual chant: "The past obliges me, the present heals me, I don't give a damn about the future."

5

TOWARD THE SEA

October 17, in Champeigne

Upon passing through the commune of Truyes, I reconnected with the trails between the fragmented forest areas, tracking the last remnants of the invisible paths. Such is the fate of beasts who must perpetually cross through endless passages of thickets. Before the advent of the stone ax by land-clearing societies, our ancestors were rather familiar with dangerous displacements where caves served as shelters: brief layovers in the middle of a forest ocean where hyenas lurked in the darkness. Then man subdued the world and the opposite evocation was posed: from that point on, it was the forest that had been transformed into fragments, and it was then up to the animals to seek out what little remained of the clusters of selva so as to hide in a wide-open landscape. A negative archipelago therefore began to materialize.

It was a flat region, softer, more familiar, less vertical than the limestone sculptures of the Vésubie, with sandy paths and reliefs like so many caresses from the palm of one's hand. I came across villages I was familiar with, falling asleep and gathering myself back up among their memories. I didn't miss the absence of the sun's striking blows on the surface of things nor the irascible air emanating in the nature of Provence. I knew I was edging closer to the sea.

The passable routes were getting a bit more complex as I entered terrains surrounded by signs saying "No trespassing." The maps I had didn't always indicate what lands were private property. I followed other tracks created by deer, but then the path would suddenly end at a barricade of bars or a sign that said, "Strictly forbidden, final notice." Holy cow! Ever since the days when Joan of Arc stood up to protect these lands, they don't kid around in the Touraine region.

When I passed by a fenced-in area with a sign announcing "Orchard under surveillance," I understood that I was entering into the orbit of the city. The city of Tours was on the horizon. Cities were like planets: their gravitational field attracted meteors, but if you got too close to them, you were bound to enter a field of turbulence. I had therefore decided to make a detour around Tours to the east. It would be enough simply to follow the Loire River by way of Vouvray and then proceed toward Monnaie.

The plateau between Indre and the departmental region of Cher was speckled with housing estates and subdivisions, warehouses and roundabouts. For two months now I had been wandering through this furniture, attempting to keep it at a distance and out of view. This time, there was no way of avoiding it. The invisible paths at least had one virtue: they snaked their way between the planned barriers for occupying the earth. Humans are somewhat peculiar in their insistence on imagining that a landscape required some form of outside planning and land management. And yet others spoke of augmented reality. One day perhaps there'll even be discussions about providing additional artificial lighting for the sun.

October 18, above the Loire River

My approach to the regional department of Cher was a real gymkhana. A real speed haul. From east to west, along the river, the railroads and national highways unfurled throughout the landscape. Veritable axons of the civilization of flux. The era's greatest preoccupation: *move fast and often*. As for me, I was traveling by foot from south to north, perpendicular to the lines of transit.

And there were going to be a lot of bridges to cross over for the next several hours!

A gaggle of hot-air balloons could be spotted in the sky out of the northwest, above the Loire. I imagined Americans floating high above, bathed in pure felicity, drinking large glasses of Chinon red, barefoot, congratulating themselves that the region had not yet been bombed.

How long did I sit hypnotized on the bridge of Montlouis by the swirling eddies of the Loire? I stared at them as they transformed into foam between the stone pylons. The river's currents were enticing to adventurers. "Was it a river of sand or a river of glory" Péguy was known to say—and called for one to jump on in (which Péguy didn't actually say). The water, having come from the massif of Auvergne, would eventually become diluted in the Atlantic Ocean. I crossed the bridge following alongside the railroad.

On the right bank of the river, the plateau of Vouvray was home to a variety of grape vines, and I knew I'd discover a friendly landscape ahead. In Provence, wine was the very lifeblood of the rock struck alchemically by the sun. Whereas here, it was a lymph of sand fertilized by endless fog. The slopes of the plateau slowly descended into cliffs pierced with caves. It was precisely the sort of alchemy that rejuvenated me: an alchemy of vines and the void. Wine had been declared off-limits. But I could still get drunk on the void.

The forest stretching to the south of Monnaie would be a welcoming landing spot for my campsite. I first had to get across the highway by way of a bridge. I stood there daydreaming, my hands stuck to the guardrails, my eyes fixated on the endless flow of automobiles. Perhaps one day, when the last drop of hydrocarbons has been used up, the ballet will finely come to an end, *subito*. And one will have to get a front-row seat, on a bridge like this, overlooking the highway: the flow will suddenly begin to come to a standstill and stop, the car doors will open, and the drivers will exit their vehicles and wave at each other, completely dumbfounded. And they will continue on foot.

I was in the woods under the last shimmers of daylight. I made a fire, set up the tiny tent that Goisque had left me, and dined under an umbrella of oak trees: I had at my disposal all the necessary elements for spending safe nights outside. The evening made the forest moan. The wheezing of the highway could be heard all the way through to the clearing. The beast knew that its days were numbered. Perpetual movement at two euros a liter couldn't go on forever.

October 19, through the region of la Gâtine tourangelle

The night turned quite noisy. I was now moving within the tourangelle forests! The leaves were falling. The forest was crackling, the trees were peeling. It was my first daybreak of white frost. The leaves of the undergrowth screeched and squealed all the way to Monnaie.

Five days followed, moving across the plains, my eyes burning after continuously squinting at a map of the landscape at 1:25,000 scale. Passing by railroads, following the edges, cutting a path under high-voltage lines, extending a salutatory greeting to every tractor I came across: tracking the invisible paths was my greatest concern and my greatest of games. In the evening, I exchanged my campsite for small, lively hotels in the city centers of various bourgs: these were my nights spent in Aubigné-Racan, Mayet, Malicorne, and Chevillé.

Sometimes, I'd even come across human beings. They were a rare sighting and always friendly. There were several of them out walking, at the periphery, carried along by dogs. At the old watermill of Fresnay, I encountered a hunting dog who afforded his master the opportunity to walk. Man was the son of places:

"I remember when the mill was still up and running. My father would bring wheat there for grinding and we would pay the miller in flour."

"And these days?" I asked.

He gave off a slightly ironic hiccup as if to wonder whether I actually thought the mill wheel was still turning to this day. In the copper-colored forests, beyond Mayet, one could make out a collection of standing stones. A series of siliceous pathways slithered their way between the pine trees to the northwest. At Saint-Martin, the local watering hole belonged to a veritable human spider. She was dressed in a black lace outfit with makeup plastered on. One asked for a cup of her juice in hopes that she would cast a spell over you. Two brothers with round heads sat at the bar imbibing their liquors, propping each other up with the tenderest of gestures. At the far wall, one could make out a myriad of creatures that had passed through the hands of a taxidermist: a stuffed owl, a crow, and a tiny garden dormouse. The chaperone left me to rest my head on the table, then returned later on and gave it a quick cleaning to help me sleep better.

October 22, in the region of Champagne mancelle

The days began to repeat themselves while the landscape continued to imperceptibly change. Only the politics of territory had imposed its slight variations. There would certainly be some sort of painting of concentric circles to sketch in the aftermath of such a walk. In the bourgs depicted in the Michelin guide, the city center was always charming, the church had been restored, and there was often a bookshop right next to the *salon de thé*. Woody Allen could easily direct his next, typical, same old film here. His actors could proclaim that *the French countryside was truly a movable feast,* and that D-Day had certainly been worth the effort.

Then the arrival of the second circle: the residential neighborhoods. A monsieur would be cutting his lawn in his pajamas. He had already finished washing his car. A poster fastened to a light pole would indicate that a local woman had passed away from Alzheimer's disease.

The third circle would then appear: the commercial sector.

The parking lot would be crammed full of automobiles and the supermarket never closed. There was a permanent sale on for ham hocks. Farther along, a roundabout provided the key directional arrows to the principal landmarks, and we made our way to the fields, the barns for parking tractors, and the woods where wild boars waited patiently for the opening of hunting season. All of this proved one thing for sure: with some effort, even a Frenchman was capable of organizing the world.

The lone downer in my day was that I was slowly getting closer to the chicken farms. There one found nothing but a concentration camp environment where suffering reigned. The chickens merely awaited death, without moving, without ever seeing the sky. A collection of beautiful cars were parked in front of these factories of living material. Someone had to profit off this concentration. My nose could no longer detect smells very well, but I could denote a slight acidic scent. Often, if I got too close to such installations, to cut across a field and make up an extra kilometer or two, the night watchmen of the areas had no problem frisking me without the least hint of humanity. Perhaps they detected a bit of the Parisian in me, quick to criticize a local country worker while having no qualms about then going outside to barbecue their own cuts of chicken breast.

On the same day, I passed above the Sarthe River (black, sensual, covered in pyrite-colored powder), the highway (which they referred to as "the Ocean"), and a new speed train route in the midst of construction whose utility I understood perfectly well: we better add another railroad line to the network in order to hurtle ourselves toward other places that we will just as quickly be in a hurry to leave.

October 24, near the region of Laval

I made my way closer to the next town and eventually entered Entrammes, where I immediately requested a Viandox from the barkeep at a café.

"What's that?" she asked.

"It's a broth," I replied.

"Never heard of it. Where can you get that?"

"Everywhere. At Brûlon, they served one to me yesterday."

"Ah, but that was in the community of Sarthe! That doesn't surprise me in the least."

La Mayenne offered up her tender paths for two days. The levee road was arranged so as to provide *a directional framework for one's life.* One had to be virtuous to undertake such tasks! From this vantage point, the barges lost a bit of their romantic nature but gained in their uprightness. It would not be a good idea to make love in the tall grasses on these paths, but one could make one's way back to Laval without leaving the riverside. I would spend an entire day lounging amidst my dreams in Laval before taking off again along the levee road following the river. The river was moving slowly and beneath its obsidian reflections, one could imagine carnivorous pike leading horrific hunts. I could see a jogger in the distance with a panicked look on her face. Upon getting one glimpse of me she had immediately made a sharp U-turn. I didn't dare look into the water to catch a glimpse of my own reflection.

At Andouillé I became interested in an innovation installed in front of the church: an "automatic bread distributor" had replaced the bakery. Put a euro in the slot and you received a baguette in return. The machine had already been vandalized. An example of French morality: When there is no more bread, the people revolt. When there are no more bakers, they break the machines.

At Chailland, a red moon rose high in an already pink sky. I rested for a bit to smoke on the railing of a bridge passing over the Ernée River. I attempted to draw the attention of passersby to the beauty of the night sky without any success. I continued to despair a bit in hopes of still encountering a soul disposed to engaging in a discussion, when, after forty kilometers of walking one evening, I arrived at La Dorée. An old man, whom I took to be a farmer, was getting a taste of fresh air against a wooden barn. He proposed that I spend the evening at his abode alongside a humid meadow. His wife was preparing crêpes. "Like in every good home in Normandy," she exclaimed, a good "helping of butter" would be spread on top of them. It was a splendid dinner in the Haute Mayenne with a lovely couple who nourished the conversation with memories.

"I was a carpenter when I got injured at the age of forty. They considered me disabled. But ten years later, my leg had healed up and I set off on the hiking trails."

"They called him 'Le vagabond,' " his wife exclaimed.

"I walked all over France for thirty years: the Alps, the Pyrenees, and the Massif Central. I passed through every region, while limping!"

"Every year he would embark on a voyage and I'd follow along behind him in a pickup truck."

"One day, I'll write a book about it. But I still have time. My father died at the age of one hundred. And I'm only eighty years old."

They spoke to me of the battles that devastated Normandy after the landings on D-Day. The counterattacks at Mortain and Falaise that they still remembered. And finally, they spoke about the fortunate and peaceful life they had made together. I thought of my own life that I couldn't quite seem to get organized at all as it flittered away while I was incapable of sealing a victory over an ongoing sense of panic. They set up a room for me to sleep in for the night. And I jotted down some notes in my book where, after some calculations, I realized I had almost walked as much as my old host, but it wasn't enough for me to simply consider that I had more time in front of me.

October 28, in the locality of Mayenne

At breakfast, as we sat and watched the morning news provide its daily distribution of nonsense, I finally understood what I liked most of all about my hosts. They didn't make any commentaries about anything. Well, they evoked the region and ended every phrase with "we really enjoy living here." In other words, they belonged to one of those rare peoples: those who kept quiet and had grown roots in a specific region.

In the hills of the Haute Mayenne, I encountered the first ambassadors from the English Channel: seagulls and hydrangea. Here, one wrapped fresh fish in pages from the *Ouest-France* newspaper, and the rooftops were made of slate: echoes that we were soon arriving at the sea. In the fog-laden background of a valley, one could make out the ruins of an abbey. I traversed through the woods, resting on the hillsides. I'd often stretch myself out to stare up and contemplate the clouds. The most pious profession in the world.

At Saint-Hilaire-du-Harcouët, the old railroad line from Ducey to Mortain would open out onto the landscape. The rails were no longer there, but the path could still be made out, heading directly west, under a viscera of foliage. A fire-red chestnut tree, well ahead of is gray-green brethren, indicated that autumn had arrived. The old brick train stations were still standing. This area was where some of the most horrible scenes from the Battle of Normandy had played out. What we considered, seventy years later, as the obvious and clear advance of the Allies, propelled forward by the cheers of the liberated people, was much rougher than predicted. "The thick, muddy quagmires of the countryside," according to the expression of the British military historian Antony Beevor, which I read again this morning in the press office, had slowed down the Anglo-American advance. Peace had returned. Along with it, the power of the forests was reestablished, and the gentleness of the green nave protected the walker at the present moment under an abundance of foliage that electrified the neck.

October 29, the bay

The path led to the bridge of Pontaubault, which had granted passage to Patton and his troops. He had initiated a perfusion of liberty by way of an umbilical cord of geography. The Sélune River, under the arches of the bridge, begrudgingly died in the silt and mud of the lagoon. Another path followed alongside the estuary close to the salty meadows near Avranches. For me, this would be the final channel, rising up to Cotentin, all the way to the Cap de la Hague, where the territory would finally collapse into the sea. I had chosen to follow the western coastline so that my left ear could enjoy the music of the breaking surf. On the other side, where the D-Day landings had taken place, I would have been deprived of the breath of the tide. Being deaf in one ear is not so bad as long as one can plan ahead to identify the places where one is going to stand. At the dinner table, at the orchestra, on peninsulas, life is always a question of positioning.

I walked calmly with tempered strides. Two months of these exercises had unleashed some sort of inner water clock–like machinery inside me that nothing could hold back. In the morning, I could still feel a piercing pain in my back. Three or four kilometers later, the pain would cease: a wheel set in motion long enough will eventually begin to oil itself. Walking also had its own alembic morality, dissolving its scoria. Each body, after it takes a fall—for the small few who are able to pick themselves back up—should go on a forced hike. Starting all the way back in Mercantour, the effort exerted had served as a kind of internal metaphysical polisher, sanding down the rough edges of my inner world. On this fine evening I would remain seated on a stone bench resting against the wall of a house, staring out at the salt-laden meadows. In front of me stood the coastline of the Cancale. To the north, there was nothing but fog from the sea up into the sky. To the south, one could make out the light of an Italian painting. It was the moment to make my devotions to walking, to my molting, to my good fortune.

On the paths of Provence, I had endured great difficulties chasing down my shadow. In the Massif Central, I had felt—deep within me—the stirring of the most infelicitous of thoughts. Here, in a world washed over with iodine, where birds crossed each other's paths wearing elegant outfits, everything seemed to be peaceful and going just fine. Everywhere I ventured, the invisible paths had bestowed on me their dual virtue: erasure of the body and a freedom of action.

A new physical disturbance had begun to afflict me for the past three days: total insomnia. The tarmac nights turned into days, and their unfair refusal to grant me sleep only enraged me even more. With one eye open, lying on the ground, I fervently awaited the prison discharge of daybreak. I would thus awaken, haggard, dress myself, and stumble out toward the next break. I immediately began to think of Cioran's nocturnal wanderings in the Bucharest of his youth. Stumbling around in the night like one of the living dead, before he had finally understood the necessity of embracing the madness granted by insomnia rather than attempting to sleep. One night upon returning home, he found his mother weeping on the couch. She had been waiting up for him for hours. She looked up at him and murmured, "I should have aborted you." Insomnia was a kind of general repetition of death without the benediction of accomplishment. My mother had in her time often dealt with this nothingness without end. As for me, I had embraced the youthful replenishment of days full of wind torrents, of friendship with the grasslands, the silhouettes of trees, the changing of the seasons, and church towers. It was certainly better than having a neurasthenic Carpathian mother!

The Sée River demarcated its angle and Mont-Saint-Michel emerged high above the grassland. The magical stupa was there before me. And the swarms of passerines exploding in the salty air tossed out their confetti for the marriage of the pagoda with the lagoon. It was the mount of the four elements. To the earth, air, and water, one could add fire, for those who maintained a steadfast faith. You have to admit that these guys from the twelfth century weren't lacking in audacity for having dared to plant their altar down right in the middle of a swamp, in front of a great big water drain, sitting in refurbished silt, the circulation of water currents, a landing site for bird migration, and the rustling of reeds! It was a glimpse of the eternal rubbing elbows with the ephemeral. But one also had to understand that the eternal resided within the gaseous exchanges in the mud, amidst the lagoon sewage and larval hatchings. The ephemeral resided in humanity's attempt to give roots to its fables on top of a pile of rocks.

An optical illusion led one's imagination to think that the reeds inverted the principles of physics: their feathers seemed to support mass. Falcons chased each other in the iodine-laden grasses. Behind the rocks, one could see the sky deploying a pearl-hued wash painting. Ah, if only Péguy had been from the Avranchin region instead of Beauce!

I crossed the Sée River and headed toward Genêts in a nervous state that I hadn't experienced in a great number of years. "My soul rose up to my skin," as Théophile Gautier used to say when he experienced something other than goosebumps. Ten years earlier I had contemplated Lhasa from an access summit at the northern edge of the city. Another time, I had pulled crosses out from an abandoned cemetery in a village of Russian fisherman in the reeds at the basin of the Aral Sea. On both these occasions, the landscape had overwhelmed me. The endless amount of physical exhaustion from walking like a wild man in both cases certainly played a role in my inner quivering.

The lone inconvenience of following the coastline between Avranches and Genêts was having Mont-Saint-Michel at my back. I had to endlessly turn around to nourish oneself with its presence. Walking suddenly became complicated, repeatedly pivoting to wave at a gigantic landmark every hundred steps. At each glance over the shoulder, the mind could regain a bit of assurance: the world still turned, the birds were still fishing, the mount remained, floating above the lagoon whose vaporous labyrinth scrambled any attempt at a concise shape. These repetitive verifications ended up giving me a stiff neck.

The wading birds were no longer out of work. Through the vegetation I could get a clear view of their ballet. I had a deep admiration for these birds. They lived and worked in layers of mud and silt, fed themselves worms while retaining an impeccable grace and a perfect cleanliness. They kept at a distance from each other, granting a bit of privacy to themselves, without ever getting too close. Can we see ourselves, us other humans, wading out into a swamp? That would be nice. I will promise to add to my bucket list the desire to be tossed out into a lagoon. I would become food for the animals—the wading birds, worms, crustaceans, and fish—and give back in the form of protein what I had snatched over the past several decades living as a carnivore. On the coastline I sliced my way through layers of silt. The recent high tides of the swamps had made the sea foam at the mouth, its saliva leaving marks on the embankment, ripping away at least 100 meters from the silt layer. And it took me much longer than expected to reach Gênets without being able to determine if it was the alluvion that had slowed me down or the compulsive gesture of grace that I continuously rendered to the silhouette of the mount.

October 30, east of Cotentin

This time, I wasn't dealing with a matter of untangling the invisible paths on the map: all one had to do was hold fast to the coastline and maintain a balance between the backwash and the silence. Daybreak opened up the heavens, drawing forth a distinct line between the earth and the clouds. Here, every sunrise could be summarized by the efforts of an oyster merchant gently splitting open the lips of a shell with his knife. Heading toward Granville, I looked out at the arrow composed of the intersection of the coastline and the horizon at least one thousand times. This gift bestowed on a man at the edge of the horizon was finally beneficial for once. The vision of this ever-changing banderilla will never leave me. The dunes collapsed, the birds got annoyed, the holly crackled by the light of its burned-out flames. The houses were equally distributed on the hills, replete with family secrets. The path snaked through the shrubs, bravely advancing toward the edge of the cliffs, regaining the backside of the dunes, destroying the ridgeline, and vanishing on the beaches. I reached Granville by evening.

I spent the following days continuing onward to the north. I found grassy hollows among the dunes to settle down for the evening. My campsite received visits from some lackadaisical rabbits who got tangled in the tensioners of my tent poles, ruining the rare moments of respite that I was able to glean in ripping myself away from insomnia. I awoke to fog-covered mornings. The beach offered itself up as a line of flight. I recalled the excitement of horses when their torsos are finally confronted with the open void. I would sometimes collapse into a brief afternoon nap on the beach grass only to be jolted awake again, hopping to my feet, obsessed with the idea of setting off again. To my left, a ribbon of sand unfolded its 200 meters of height. Traversing this same area of coastline on the eastern side, one June 6, caused the death of ten thousand soldiers. They ran toward the dunes, cut down by fire and steel. Seventy years later, I walked gently across the same beach peacefully along the white strands.

I retained a respect for the incursions the sea inflicted on the land. In making a detour around the lagoon (*havre* in the Norman language), I had to tack on an additional 12 kilometers to find myself right back in front of the point I had left. I renewed a certain kinship with those voyagers of the fjords, battling it out with the efforts imposed on them by the Scandinavian coastlines. On passing each swamp, one could hear the gurgling of the canals siphoning water from the lagoons. The boats remained still, their keels firmly planted, as they awaited the reversal of the flows. The sea left behind several shards of stained glass. It had to make good on its payment in the form of reflections of the sky. Fishermen could be seen cleaning their tarps, equipped with their fishnets that aided them in catching shrimp or other shellfish. These folks would certainly be resistant to future crises. Whitened by layers of salt, the grass waited for the water to return to provide its rejuvenating forces. These were blessed sites, embracing the air and water, darkness and the sun. Life on earth was born in such basins where bacteria splashed about within the alternance of elements.

On the edges of the harbors, mops of reeds obscured the horizon. It was vegetation made for an ambush. In his *Chevalier des touches,* Barbey d'Aurevilly had depicted a number of encounters of the antirevolutionary resistance behind these curtains of "shrubs and straw." Hiding behind gorses, refractory priests of the Sacré Coeur fought for the king.

Barbey d'Aurevilly used the term *chouanner*—making a verb out of the reference to the Chouan brothers of the counterrevolution—to denote the action of his Norman heroes. Under his pen, the term signified both refusing new doctrines as well as leading one's guerilla campaign in lace, circulating in the shadows, living hidden by imitating the cries of animals, defending a world behind the levees and the slopes. And such races, where one played both a serious and a leisurely game, were they not the perfect incarnation of a life on the invisible paths? To revive this peculiar term all one had to do was transpose the techniques of running out in the wooded countryside onto one's personal life. I was sure other mad worlds were still in existence. Behind all the movements of the interior terrain, there were still acres of sun and wide-open beaches.

November 3, on the coastline

I avoided the seaside resorts by taking short detours on the beach. The sand was speckled with a million twists expelled by the worms. This lent the saltmarshes a resemblance to Southeast Asian rice fields. The harbors adorned the coastline at a slower pace than the postwar accumulation of vacation villages. I passed by Pirou-Plage, Lindbergh-Plage, Barneville-Plage. All these installations were projections of old historical villages onto the seafront where the land had receded several kilometers inland from the coast. During their reconstruction, the leisure society had left its mark in reshaping the landscape. After the grain silo and the highway bypass, the seaside resort constituted one of the singular totems of a prosperous France. The societies of the 1960s, certain of the future, transformed the territory into a playground. To the east, along the alpine ridge, one could see the myriad ski resorts constructed to attract vacationers to winter sports. Six months later, the scales tilted in the other direction and led summer vacationers to the seaside. So it was that "leisure basecamps" were formed along with "vacation villages." One played on the beaches raked by tractors before then sliding on top of powder spit out by snow canons. The *geography of leisure* had dealt the final necessary scalpel blows for attenuating the transformation of the face of the country. Deserted during the tourist offseason, these sites resembled the charm of theater corridors where stage managers stored the sets. The only people moving about on the beach were the fishermen, maneuvering their machinery, cultivating their seashell gardens during low tide. Sometimes, a dog would cross the road. Upon the return of summer, the bell from the ice cream vendor would ring out to signal the return of men to the coast, pleading once again with the sea to reinvigorate their bleached white bodies after months spent in the cities.

November 5

The path regained its fraternal dispositions, cutting a serpentine trail out of the void, brushing up against the extremity of Cape Carteret on the narrow ridge of the cliffs. The sea churned its froth against the black reef flats. The inlets led one to guess who might be hiding there: the Chouan brothers or one of Barbey d'Aurevilly's old mistresses. A salty, prickly flora clung to the void, resisting with admirable modesty. They provided a lesson to alpinists lost at the edge of the Norman world.

Goisque and Humann had met back up with me at Barneville-Carteret, and we set up our tents facing the Anglo-Norman islands, on the overhang of Cap du Rozel, protected by the stone walls that were themselves crowned with yellow broom flowers. The plots of land bore a name that suited the campsite of the sentinels: *le corps de garde.* Clouds, and then the night, formed a mask over the islands. Beginning at daybreak, Goisque, covered in photographic apparatuses, was determined not to let the slightest reflection from the English Channel escape his lens. As for Humann, he was wondering why we were so enamored of Cotentin when there was Crimea to explore. As for me, I found it rather inconsiderate to have traveled the world over without exploring the treasures in one's own backyard.

Goisque admitted that he might be experiencing a form of mental disorganization by the fact that he was having flashbacks to the Kuril Islands even though we had just come from Cambrai.

"If I were the dictator of France," Humann added, "I would make every child walk across the entire country. It would serve as a preventive to obesity, and everyone would learn the names of all the plants."

"And the politicians!" exclaimed Goisque. "Their election would be decided by who could walk several weeks in a row without stopping! It would certainly provoke a Lazarus effect."

I was slowing down my friends by spending too much time contemplating the stone walls. The art of bocage marquetry had attained a high level of refinement. The stones welcomed the moss. The moss rounded out the angles and protected societies from wildlife. Oh, what a splendid form of saving grace to be able to propose a "political theory of the bocage" as a cure to the convulsions of the world! We would be inspired by the ingenuity of hedges. They separated without walling things off, demarcated without rendering opaque, protected without repelling. Air passed through them, birds created their nests in them, and fruit grew around them. One could easily traverse them, but they also served to prevent landslides. In their shadows, life flourished. In their interconnected knotworks, worlds prospered; behind their lace, plots of land were deployed. The medusa of the recent rise of globalism had swallowed up the bocage areas. This land consolidation of the global theater announced the arrival of a new era. It would perhaps be an era of happiness, but that's not the impression that seemed to resonate from it. Who knew whether the new planetary savannas would create forums of happiness or new battlefields? The only thing that was certain was that a storm was making its way into Flamanville and we needed to seek shelter. And there was no megalithic structure in sight! Not one bunker! Not even a watering hole high up on the cliff.

Hobbling along on the invisible paths had led me to a country that didn't seem to be very well disposed to the changing times. It's perhaps a bit unfair to make accusations against a country that bears the weight of ages. How can a country like France make successful strides forward in an era of globalization when it is still attached to an old notion of its claim to some archaic destiny? A fossil is never mature enough for its metamorphosis. Do we ask the preservationist of the hall of treasures his opinion about international affairs? From the tropical zones all the way to the Arctic of Greenland, we can see the emergence of nations prepared to be the new planetary station agents and global grocers. For us, who still maintain a belief of being at the center of the world, invested with a global mission of universalism, globalization was not a good bargain. From the very beginning, the countryside suffered incredible mutations. The farmers made their consternation manifest in the face of a market that took on the dimensions of the globe. And we could understand their malaise: when one had cultivated a land for more than two thousand years, it was not an easy task to embrace participating in the global trade show.

Light pierced and covered the Bay of Sciotot with a moiré pattern. The rain was not intimidated and returned rather quickly. The afternoon came and went under an anthracite-colored sky as I snuck a couple of quick glimpses of La Hague nuclear plant. Sometimes, we would seek refuge in a village café. In Normandy, one's principal preoccupation was always finding a seat on the proper side of the windowpane.

We arrived at Diélette by way of a labyrinth of tiny stone walls. The sea bore the color of wet limestone. There was a myriad of homes opposite a succession of promising store fronts that we passed dreaming of the wooden parquets and polished furniture inside. In one of the more elaborate gardens in the village some jokesters had planted a stele bearing the inscription: "To the anonymous radiation victims." It was a reference to the recycling of nuclear waste. At the hotel, however, I was quite happy to finish the end of *Le chevalier des touches* under the light of my head lamp.

November 6, toward the Cape

I opened my maps to verify the location of the Cap de la Hague, the final leg of my journey. The nose of Jobourg plunged into the department of the Manche. The upper portion of the map contained nothing but a large swath of deep blue, indicating that I was nearing the end of my long walk. I attempted to place something ceremonious into the final folds of the map. After all, this gesture would conclude my slow undertaking of reconstruction. Instead, I was interrupted by a great gust of wind.

The Cotentin Peninsula was something like the left arm of France stretched out over the ocean, waiting to see if it encountered a drop of water, so as to get a sense of whether or not it was raining. The dunes of Biville slowly formed between the bocages and the sea. They bore a pastel vegetation. Was there some form of respect undertaken by the vegetation in regard to the sky so as not to allow the slightest bit of loud color to emerge in this region?

That evening, we set up our drenched tents at a campsite on the nose of Jobourg. The lights emanating from the central nuclear power plant recalled the fact that one had to really be a complete imbecile to set up a campsite out in the rain during the era of atomic fission.

November 7

I waited to be liberated by the arrival of daylight. For the insomniac, each dawn is like one's own personal June 6. To the east, a leaden sky torn apart by solar glory: this was the image that appeared through the tent opening. Rays of light appeared to shoot out silver coins onto the surface of the waters below. Ferns velveted the hills. The morning forecast looked good. Ten thousand years ago, hunter-gatherers had struggled on these very escarpments to nourish themselves in order to survive. The Normans referred to these areas as the "highlands"; these same tiny slopes would have incited laughter in the inhabitants of the Savoy region. The peoples of the reindeer should be lauded, however, for standing strong and fighting it out on the land instead of engaging with an even more savage sea. Ten thousand years later, the installations of European pressurized water reactors now decorated the landscape, their antennas shooting up into the sky far and wide. We had gone from carving bone to modifying the atom. Time passed. The sky remained gray.

The vegetation on the guard rails was rather valiant. Broom flowers and wild teasel grew up above the void. Wind gusts twisted the shrub bushes without displacing them. Perhaps they suffered from being ripped apart by thorns. Shrubs are to the slopes what livestock herders were to these environs: brave, stubborn, on the edge of the Western world.

Each replacement on the path cut a new thread into the somber ridgeline. Crows settled into kelp before flying away, having been disturbed by a breath. In Norman mythology, crows incarnated figures of memory. Here, they watched over the old granite rocks that had been roughed up by the perpetual rising swells. Guardians of memories, witnesses to ancient shipwrecks. We finally arrived at the lighthouse at Goury: *a hellscape* occupied by a lighthouse keeper up until the 1990s, before the advent of automated-electrical systems.

Humann pondered an interesting thought: "Is hell merely a place where one lives entirely alone?"

November 8, the Edge of the Map and the End of the Territory

We were walking toward the Nez Bayard under a sunrise teeming with seagulls. On the opposite side, German bunkers could be seen crumbling in the prairies. We sat down and propped ourselves up against a tiny wall. This was the most septentrional point on the Cotentin Peninsula. I had arrived at the semaphore of La Hague.

While bedridden, I had dreamt of setting out on this walk across France. I had raised myself back up to accomplish it, and now it was coming to completion. It was a voyage born from a fall. Some of the paths and routes had been sufficiently solitary and labyrinthian to suit my tastes. The scent of hawthorn and fresh bark still lingered in the air. I had accompanied my walk with several stumbles. My arrival at the end largely consisted of staying close to the railings so as to settle up my accounts and forget all past misfortunes. From now on, new invisible paths would open themselves up on the horizon: beyond simply glancing down at a map at 1:25,000 scale, my task would be to invent them. A strategy of withdrawal. Flights, retreats, gentle steps along the coast, long absences burdened with silence and fed on visions.

Every long walk has its moments of salvation. We set out on the road, we make our way forward by seeking out perspectives in the bramble and avoiding the village. We seek out shelter for the evening. We reimburse ourselves in the form of dreams composed from the sadness of the day. We take up residence in the forest, fall asleep cradled by the owls, depart again the next morning, rejuvenated by the madness of the tall grass where we cross paths with horses. We encounter silent farmers.

Rural France maintains itself within its withdrawal. Elsewhere, it ebbs. One swamp gives way to another. History had transformed this territory into an elaborate and laborious chessboard. Its remains could still be uncovered. The farmers and workers in the countryside bid their farewell to a world whose substitute they knew nothing about. The conversations with the men I encountered were never that long. They had other things to do with their time.

When we headed back out into the fields, inexplicably, we saw the apparition of the faces of our mothers, right at the crossroads of paths in the middle of the forest. Heading back out into the fallow land and settling back into the woods we perceived beautiful stone chapels; we walked alongside rivers, then on the coastline we walked on the sand and we could hear the backwash, and we finally ended up at the edge of the country. And so, one then simply heads back home, finally rid of the insect that had taken a bite out of one's heart. And all the pain eventually washes away, and one is set back upright on one's two feet.

One must still respond to the invitations made by maps, believe in their promises, cross entire countries, and stand there for a couple of minutes so as to close out a bad chapter in one's life.

I spent one last night on a grassy rock, on my way to the peninsula, right outside Omonville-la-Rogue. We reached our location in the dark, on top of slippery rocks. We set up our tents and the noise of the cresting waves kept sleep at bay. Today, we had knocked out thirty-five kilometers by complicating our route a bit within the bocages.

"It's done," I exclaimed.

Fate had granted me the grace to walk again as much as I wanted and to sleep under the stars at livable outposts: among plateaus of wall faces, undergrowth, and cliff edges. The country was there, beneath my feet. No one truly knows what will lead them to engage in a metamorphosis. Nations are not reptiles: they have no prescience as to what will be done with their shed skin. France's appearance was different. The countryside's face had changed. The form of its cities had changed, and the swamp rose around our tent. Tomorrow, we wouldn't be able to dawdle. We had learned at least one thing: we could still depart straight ahead in front of ourselves and struggle with nature. There were still valleys where we could fill entire days without laying our eyes on another single person to tell us which direction to take. And we could crown these hours battling it out with the wind at night in the most grandiose of retreats. All we had to do was seek them out. Interstices still existed. Invisible paths remained. We had nothing to complain about.

AFTERWORD

A Lesson in the Art of Dreaming

Drew S. Burk

*The wildwood brings on a mild nostalgia, not for home
or place, but for lost innocence—the paradise lost that, as
Proust said, is the only paradise.*

PETER MATTHEISSEN

The world reveals itself to those who travel on foot.

WERNER HERZOG

For those readers who have not had the good fortune of reading
the vast oeuvre of Sylvain Tesson, this present work perhaps will
serve as an entryway into a fantastic realm halfway into the terra
incognita of a travel writer and adventurer as we meet him in the
midst of returning home and healing from a near-fatal fall from a
roof. In his home country of France, the work of Sylvain Tesson
has garnered a large readership and his love of climbing buildings as well as mountains—even free-climbing up the side of the
Notre-Dame Cathedral in Paris as well as hiking Mount Everest—
has made him a sort of literary legend within his own time. The
writer of *In Praise of Vagabond Energy,*[1] who once described the
absurd cosmic relation between humans and fossil fuels, traveling
by bicycle alongside a pipeline traversing the vast open landscape

of the Far East and the arid desert of the former Soviet Union, imbibing the local cultures of others and the mysteries of humanity's reliance on the dead, will have to confront, in mourning the death of his mother and his own severe accident, the question of how to begin again.

Seeking a way to heal himself through the very activity of walking and confronting the land that he had once mostly sought to leave, our author would also have to reconcile his own mode of living life as a literary enfant terrible. Once nourishing himself on books alone, forgetting the need to temper his relation with the written word, he promises himself to set out on a walk, forgetting what other authors he once worshipped in his youth have recounted. "To rejoice in the sun without feeling the need to evoke de Staël. To partake in the comforting embrace of the wind without citing Hölderlin." He would therefore have to take leave for a time from those writers whose work had nourished him as a younger writer. He would instead seek to return or reflect briefly on the very modes of living of other respected writers, such as the French botanist Jean Fabre and Provençal novelist Jean Giono,[2] who were creatures of their locales, hardly traveling much at all yet giving themselves over, each in his own way, to the literary and written form by way of a relation with the surrounding earth. And more particularly in vital communion with the cosmic universe— with all the creatures and primary, elemental flows of life.

What had gone wrong in the machinery of globalization that ignored the local for an absurd relation to the technological affordances of accelerated global production that were ecologically deleterious? A practice where, as the author laments, one's toothbrush had more than likely traveled the globe before arriving at one's local general store. A machinery thanks to which even the most peaceful and important of human activities common to all people that once granted a sense of community—making the daily journey to one's corner bakery to obtain a baguette for dinner—had now become automated.

This work is, in part, a lesson about practices of meditation and dreaming. Of course, we could say it's about hiking and camping for one hundred days. But that would be to miss something of much more vital import, the nuance of ritual and reverence to nature and to life. To partake in the solar star and the wind, to set off on a voyage of self-knowledge through movement alone within nature, communing with the silent shepherds and moving up at high altitudes along ancient monastical enclaves and pagan sites of worship. Wandering among the ruins and rubble as ancient as the land itself. "The walker is not worthy of what he treads upon." And yet our author walks.

. . .

We begin to understand what sort of spiritual journey our author has embarked upon, when, after days of walking up into the mountains, he encounters several monks in a monastery on a cliff edge who suggest he pay a visit to a hermit named Lucien, yet higher up on a mountain ridge, who is in the midst of reading one of the author's own earlier works about residing for six months in solitude in a cabin on Lake Baikal.[3] The feverish dreamer, living off books and stale bread, becomes just one of a myriad of doubles—shadow figures—our author must overcome and, perhaps in his own way, pay respects to throughout his journey. As if to assuage himself as well and forgo part of his past, he offers up to the hermit his own beloved copy of De Quincey's *Confessions of an English Opium Eater.* And we are provided then, from the beginning, a sign that this journey will be one about reckoning with humanity's relation to excess—as much literary as materially within the landscape—in the way humankind manages and restrains itself from the excess of its own technological innovations.

Sylvain Tesson is well versed in such forms of spiritual reverie that have been practiced for millennia by monks and wanderers, shamans and ascetics. The art of wandering without destination, *destinerrance,* implies such a reflection as well. As paradoxical as it may seem, it requires returning to that ancient adage, attributed to many a sage and teacher, of knowing thyself, but only through attention to setting off in movement—both inward and outward—to take up a profound practice of solitude, oftentimes out in nature, that hikers, cyclists, and long-distance trail runners in our current era know well. The rurality Tesson seeks to understand in part also resides within such a temporality. Where the daily relation to ritual and routine—to bread making, cheese making, the cultivation of lavender, and other forms of artisanal crafts—is still practiced. A slower pace was calling out to our author.

For Tesson, one can do no better than to regain a sense of quietude and reverence for the earth and the other forms of the living by quietly walking along what he refers to as the *invisible paths.* Paths that are not encumbered by highways or noise pollution of city centers and acres of pavement serving to only exacerbate climate change, but rather pathways such as the *restanques,* the stone steps of Provence that lead one up and down in elevation alongside ancient paths through the Cévennes, or the meditative footpaths found on the sacred pilgrimage along the ancient Compostela route.

The destination, in these instances, is largely to take back up the practice, again and again, of what in Japanese is referred to as a *kata,* as a form of sacred ritual whereby one can partake of community and solitude within an inner relation and exploration of self, if only to forgo too much self-reflection, so as to regain and retain one's focus and attention on the very task at hand: *to be in the present.*

In this case, the kata becomes the daily repetition and routine, the very attention to wandering alongside rivers and hiking up mountain ridges, seeking at times a clearing for making his nightly campfire and settling down to sleep. And the more he practices the ritual, the more he traverses a different relation to time and space. At once waking from one dream and yet evermore plunging into another. He is only awoken from his slumber in part by the strangers he encounters along the various paths: other vagabonds and Roma, farmers and hikers, homesteaders from other European countries, American cyclists, and even Legionnaires. And in this manner, our wounded traveler slowly heals himself by way of a kind of ambulatory meditation.

Since this work was first written, Sylvain Tesson has gone on to take an active interest in the reconstitution and preservation of more than seventy thousand additional hectares of old-growth forests throughout France and bordering European countries. Perhaps it is best to reflect on what we can learn from the presence of trees—those ancient, silent beings that represent such an essential resource for all of us. Such, it would seem, would be, in the end, the vital spiritual reflection that one is offered when one seeks to commune with life in the forest and that Tesson wishes to share and rediscover, in his own manner, with the reader of this work: to put some essential supplies in a backpack, head out on a walk under a quiet tree canopy or alongside a river, and spend an afternoon gazing out at the flowing water, basking in the wind currents, and slowly following him on his voyage of discovery on the wandering paths, "between walls composed of books and forest trails."

NOTES

1. Starting Off on the Wrong Foot

1. Sylvain Tesson, *The Consolations of the Forest: Alone in a Cabin on the Siberian Taiga,* trans. Linda Coverdale (New York: Rizzoli Ex Libris, 2013).

2. Of Ruins and Brambles

1. The reader should note that the author here is referring to Flaubert's famous travelogue, *Pars les champs et par les grèves,* translated into English as *Over Strand and Field,* in which Flaubert sets out on a journey with a friend through Brittany. In the context of the author's comments, there is a dual meaning available to the French reader that merits a brief explanation for the English-language reader. The word play centers largely on the term *grève,* which, in contemporary French, refers more commonly to the notion of "a workers strike." Such a reflection in part serves as a historical trajectory that the author seeks to understand within the contemporary context throughout the rest of the work. How a sense of the rural or the countryside that was once a common part of one's relation to place and one's psychic development gave way to an increasing urbanization of land management and also potentially to a more docile conception and praise of the cityscape and governmental obedience through city infrastructure as opposed to the open expanse of the fields, which, for the author, are tied to a sense of freedom and the rural. Such in part is the paradoxical paradigm of freedom and convenience that the author seeks to reflect on throughout the work in regard to increasing urbanization,

the subsequent need for more housing, and the ongoing land management of infrastructure as well as the digital technological development of the landscape that throughout the course of the early twenty-first century will move from the material landscape into the immaterial landscape of digital culture.—Trans.

2. Prioritized Urban Zones [*Zones à urbaniser en priorité*] were created during the 1950s and 1960s to provide an increase in both housing and commercial development, including the creation of entire neighborhoods and urban areas. The ZUP project largely corresponded to a global housing shortage combined with the postwar era of the baby boom and was often done in such as manner as to standardize the areas created; a lack of dynamism was often criticized. *Zone d'aménagement concerté,* or ZAC, was a law passed in 1967 to address other forms of the urban management of space.—Trans.

3. Giogio Agamben, *What Is an Apparatus?,* trans. David Kishik and Stefan Pedatella (Stanford, Calif.: Stanford University Press, 2009).

4. The French term *oraison* is understood as well as the notion of a funerary prayer.—Trans.

5. *Les Trente Glorieuses,* or *Glorious Thirty,* was the name given to the postwar period from 1945 to 1975 in France. It was considered a time of great prosperity, economic production, and infrastructural growth.—Trans.

6. J. Barbey d'Aurevilly, *Premier Memorandum (1836–38)* (Paris: Alphonse Lemerre, 1900), 1. "Cela duera le temps qu'il plaira à Dieu, c'est à dire l'ennui, qui est bien le dieu de ma vie."

7. The French term couleuvre can denote both a snake and "a tall tale."—Trans.

8. It may be of interest to the reader that the author's offhand remark about "Roy's Rest Stop," after declaring he could be sovereign only over himself, more than likely refers to medieval French orthography for *the king—le Roy*—as opposed to the everyday appellation of *le roi.* Staying for the night at "Roy's Rest Stop" could therefore be considered a lighthearted recollection that at one point in history, all forested areas were considered under ownership of the king. And yet, perhaps "Roy" in this instance might also be a reference to Monsieur Le Roy, the king's gardener at Versailles, also considered, by some, the first gardener and conservationist of France. Moving from the wilderness back into civilization by spending a night in a

hotel could therefore be, in the author's quixotic manner, a way to establish an eloquent history as well as a geography lesson. Whether he is referring to himself as the ruler of his own kingdom or to the medieval king or the king's gardener, he grants to the reader a brief insight into the shift from feudalism to individual land ownership and, in the process, both a historical and a geographical reflection on the notion of territory, civilization, and the wilderness, in regard to a time when land could not yet be owned by individuals nor conserved by the state but rather a time when the first conservationist was either the king, le Roy, or Monsieur Le Roy, the king's gardener. For more on this subject see the magisterial work by Robert Pogue Harrison, *Forests: The Shadow of Civilization* (Chicago: University of Chicago Press, 1992).—Trans.

3. The Invisible Paths

1. Alphonse de Lamartine, "Isolation," trans. Peter Shor. http://www-math.mit.edu/~shor/Isolement.html.
2. Cédric Gras, *L'Hiver aux trousses* (Paris: Stock, 2015).
3. A reference to the more ancient name of the region derived from the Gaballi, one of many Gallic tribes.—Trans.
4. The author uses the term *puech*, thereby allowing access to a larger linguistic expanse of the territory he's traversing. "Pitch" is derived from the Occitan word *puèg*, coming from the Latin *ped*, which yields the term *podium* and is transcribed into the transcription into French as *puech*. It is still commonly used in a specific region of France to refer to certain mountain summits. https://fr.wikipedia.org/wiki/Puech_(montagne).

4. The Invisible Shadows

1. Henri-Alain Fournier, *The Lost Estate* (*Le Grand Meaulnes*), trans. Robin Buss, intro. Adam Gopnik (New York: Penguin Classics, 2007).
2. Emile Combes studied to become a priest but abandoned his studies and instead became a Freemason and then, later, a statesman. He was primarily known as a leading advocate and driving force for the separation of church and state, as well as the implementation of daily working hour limits on miners and other working-class groups. He was considered a spiritualist and was often referred to as "le petit père" or "little Father" owing to his enforcement of the

separation of church and state, in particular in regard to the closing of church schools. He was considered as an ardent anticleric positioned on the Social Democratic left of the French Third Republic.—Trans.

3. See Élisabeth Barillé, *L'oreille d'or* (Paris: Grasset, 2016).

Afterword

1. Sylvain Tesson, *Éloge de l'énergie vagabonde* (Paris: Éditions des Équateurs, 2007).
2. Jean Giono, *The Man Who Planted Trees,* 20th anniversary ed. (White River Junction, Vt.: Chelsea Green Publishing, 2007).
3. Sylvain Tesson, *The Consolations of the Forest*, trans. Linda Coverdale (New York: Penguin Press, 2013).

A UNIVOCAL BOOK

Drew S. Burk, Consulting Editor

Univocal Publishing was founded by Jason Wagner and Drew S. Burk as an independent publishing house specializing in artisanal editions and translations of texts spanning the areas of cultural theory, media archeology, continental philosophy, aesthetics, anthropology, and more. In 2017, Univocal ceased operations as an independent publishing house and became a series with its publishing partner, the University of Minnesota Press.

Univocal Authors

Miguel Abensour
Judith Balso
Jean Baudrillard
Philippe Beck
Simon Critchley
Fernand Deligny
Jacques Derrida
Vinciane Despret
Georges Didi-Huberman
Jean Epstein
Vilém Flusser
Barbara Glowczewski
Évelyne Grossman
Félix Guattari
Olivier Haralambon
David Lapoujade
François Laruelle
David Link
Sylvère Lotringer

Jean Malaurie
Michael Marder
Serge Margel
Quentin Meillassoux
Friedrich Nietzsche
Peter Pál Pelbart
Jacques Rancière
Lionel Ruffel
Felwine Sarr
Michel Serres
Gilbert Simondon
Étienne Souriau
Isabelle Stengers
Sylvain Tesson
Eugene Thacker
Antoine Volodine
Elisabeth von Samsonow
Siegfried Zielinski

Sylvain Tesson has walked from Russia to India, participated in archaeological digs in Afghanistan and Pakistan, and wintered alone in a cabin on a lake in Siberia. He earned a diplôme d'études apliquées in physical geography from the University of Paris VIII. One of France's most celebrated writers, he has been awarded the Prix Médicis and the Prix Goncourt de la nouvelle. He is author of *The Consolations of the Forest* and *The Art of Patience: Seeking the Snow Leopard in Tibet,* which won the 2019 Prix Renaudot.

Drew S. Burk has edited and translated contemporary works of continental philosophy, art history, the philosophy of aesthetics, and the environmental humanities by thinkers as diverse as Georges Didi-Huberman, François Laruelle, Judith Balso, and Felwine Sarr. He is a consulting editor for the Univocal series with the University of Minnesota Press and continues to wander on foot and by bicycle.

Daniel Hornsby is the author of *Via Negativa* and *Sucker*. He lives in Minneapolis and teaches creative writing at Macalester College.